C000272835

Strengthening Mental Health Through Effective Career Development

A Practitioner's Guide

Strengthening Mental Health Through Effective Career Development:
A Practitioner's Guide.
Copyright© Dave E. Redekopp and Michael Huston, Life-Role Development
Group Ltd. (2020)

www.life-role.com

Developed with the support of

Published by:
CERIC
Foundation House
Suite 300, 2 St. Clair Avenue East
Toronto, ON M4T 2T5
Website: www.ceric.ca
Email: admin@ceric.ca

ISBN
Paperback: 978-1-988066-43-1
ePUB: 978-1-988066-44-8
ePDF: 978-1-988066-45-5

Design and layout: Jo-Anna Sharun, Untitled Ink on Paper

This material may be used, reproduced, stored, or transmitted for non-commercial
purposes. However, the authors' copyright is to be acknowledged. It is not to be
used, reproduced, stored, or transmitted for commercial purposes without written
permission from CERIC. Every reasonable effort has been made to identify the
owners of copyright material reproduced in this publication and to comply with
Canadian Copyright law. The publisher would welcome any information regarding
errors or omissions.

Contents

AUSTRALIAN CENTRE FOR
CAREER EDUCATION

CERIC | Advancing Career Development in Canada | Promouvoir le développement de carrière au Canada

Life-Role Development Group Ltd.
NOW | NEXT | FUTURE

SFU | FACULTY OF EDUCATION

Acknowledgements

Everyone in the career development field knows that nobody works entirely alone. We were able to conceive, start writing, continue writing, finish writing (including re-writing our so-called "finished writing" after getting valuable feedback) and then happily see it go through the process of layout/design, e-formatting, printing, and distribution only because of the encouragement, support, and feedback we received from many people and organizations. We name many of them below in full knowledge that some important people are missing: the ones who posted a tweet that then connected us with someone else; who came up to us after a talk and said "Keep at this—you're onto something here;" who asked supportive questions during a conference session; who gave us an idea to pursue or an article to consult. We thank the dozens of encouragers even if we do not name them.

CERIC, a significant grantor of the book, provided funds and, more importantly, their marketing and publishing expertise. It could be that the book would have been written without them, but a copy of it may never have seen the light of anyone's bookshelf beyond our own. Thank you to Riz Ibrahim, Sharon Ferriss, and Norman Valdez.

The Faculty of Education at Simon Fraser University, via Kris Magnusson, provided a significant contribution in the form of funding a research assistant, Rachel Moxham, whose insightful and articulate contribution helped us to mine the evidence base in the realm of career development and mental health.

Australia's Career Education Association of Victoria (CEAV), represented by Bernadette Gigliotti, contributed funds, feedback, and advice on accommodating language and career development approaches to ensure a suitable fit with our Australian colleagues. Bernadette also arranged a two-day conference on career development and mental health in two locations in Victoria, Australia.

On the moral support front, we thank Christa Boychuk who, before we even had a book in mind, sent many articles our way about mental illness and career development. Likewise, many thanks to Jack Dobbs, whose vision, insight, and heartfelt encouragement contributed significantly to our initial explanatory models of career development as mental health intervention. We also thank the late Frans Meijers, who asked us to write a paper on this topic for a special edition of the British Journal of Guidance & Counselling; conference organizers at the Alberta Career Development Conference, Canadian Counselling and Psychotherapy Association Conference, Cannexus, and Contact Conference, who allowed us to test out new ideas with discerning audiences; Paula Wischoff-Yerama and the board of the Career Development Association of Alberta, who organized a four-city workshop tour; Alastair MacFadden, Christa Ross, and Judy Brown, who organized a six-city workshop series for Saskatchewan's Ministry of Immigration and Career Training; and particularly career development practitioners in the provinces of Alberta and Saskatchewan in Canada and the state of Victoria in Australia for helping us refine our ideas, test practices, and become continually re-energized.

With regard to the book's content and its articulation, thank you to the following reviewers of drafts (some quite rough!):

- Andrew Culberson, Learning Specialist, Universal Design for Career Education, Education Support Services, New Brunswick Education and Early Childhood Development
- Trisha Kurylowich, Career and Employment Consultant, Peace River, Alberta
- Don MacInnis, Organization Development Consultant, Calgary, Alberta
- Peter Robertson, Associate Professor/Head of Social Sciences, Edinburgh Napier University, Edinburgh, Scotland
- Mark Slomp, Executive Director, Student Services, Student Affairs, University of Lethbridge, Lethbridge, Alberta
- Joanne Webber, Director, Disability Inclusion PTY LTD and Consultant, Building Ability through Career Management Project, CEAV, Melbourne, Victoria

We are also very grateful to Dimitra Chronopoulos, whose efficient and skilled editing significantly improved and refined our initial work.

We are indebted to the late Bryan Hiebert, whom we both met when he was with the University of Calgary and with whom we both worked in different capacities over the years. Bryan's insistence on clarity and parsimony has touched much of what we do, but it his work on controlling stress that is foundational to this book. His approach to stress control was ahead of its time. We are grateful that we have stayed in the field long enough to finally understand its value.

We are grateful as well to the people with whom we share our home lives: Dave's family, Cathy and Maya, and Michael's family, Stacey, Hayley, and James. To say that they have noticed our absence, in mind if not body, would be an understatement. Their support and patience as we navigated trips, trainings, early conference calls, and a cascading series of deadlines has made it all workable, easier, and fun.

To us [Aboriginal and Torres Strait Islander Peoples of Australia], health is about so much more than simply not being sick. It's about getting a balance between physical, mental, emotional, cultural and spiritual health. Health and healing are interwoven, which means that one can't be separated from the other.

Dr. Tamara Mackean

To Ponder...

Think of a client or student you have worked with whose life seemed significantly and positively altered by the career development work they did with you. Take a mental inventory of the changes you witnessed.

1. Introduction: Finding Our Place in the Mental Health Movement

We both know and remember clients whose lives have changed as a result of their participation in a career development process, workshop, or course. In truth, the heart of this book is captured in client stories, both those we have witnessed personally and those practitioners have recounted to us during a training activity. In our direct work with clients, there are many stories:

- Students who felt "normal" and less stressed after they learned about career decision-making and recognized that they were part of the majority of students worried about their future, uncertain what to do, and doubting they will make it.
- Individuals who recovered and relaunched after the devastation of job loss with a sense of confidence and personal optimism about managing their future in a complex labour market.
- Clients with different capacities who believed they would never find a rewarding place in the labour market, but who, after

discovering or developing particular strengths, were able to find and maintain meaningful employment.

- Employees who felt aimless and disillusioned at work (and carried this ennui home to their families) who gained a spring in their step after recognizing ways they could fulfil their values and interests outside of work, move a little closer to their preferred futures, and develop their capacity within upcoming projects at work.

Both of us have always had a sense of the connection between mental health and career development. Some thought leaders (Brown & Brooks, 1985; Herr, 1989; Super, 1957) had written about this topic years ago, but somehow our field did not pursue this thread. The last decade has seen the rise of a global mental health movement that implicates institutions, organizations, schools, managers, employees, and parents in recognizing, supporting, and intervening with mental health. Mental health is now everyone's business. The thought leaders' words and thousands of client stories told us that career development had a place in supporting positive mental health, but it had been lost in the frenzy of the mental health movement.

In 2012, we had been facilitating a training event with career development practitioners in Medicine Hat, Alberta, Canada. We usually debrief over dinner when on the road. After discussing the day and what we would do the next day, we caught up on our respective lives and shared stories about our activities away from the training road show. Legitimizing career development work and providing stakeholders (funders, managers, and administrators) with reasons to fund or support it is a recurring theme for most career development practitioners and it usually comes up when we discuss our work. Over dinner, we again discussed this theme. This time, though, was different. We both had stories of support for career services being displaced by a focus on mental health—stories of well-intentioned administrators either considering or choosing to invest in mental health intervention and consequently to reduce investment in and commitment to career development.

We get it. Resources are finite, and it makes sense to invest in areas that will make the most difference to the most people. Our stories told us that the shift in support from career development to mental health was misguided. Challenging it would require evidence that career intervention was, in fact, mental health intervention. We thought it would be easy to find this evidence; according to Dave's now-famous quote from that dinner, "It ought to be like shooting fish in a bucket." Neither of us has ever shot fish in a bucket so we don't actually know if it is easy. If it is, then it is nothing like showing evidence for a connection between career development intervention and mental health outcomes. Despite the difficulty, we have stayed with the topic, and this book is a summary of our work in the area since.

As a career development practitioner, we know you have watched many clients[1] transform. They come into your service or classroom lethargic, emotionally flat, tentative, and reactive. At some point—maybe while reviewing their strengths, clarifying their preferred future, researching work possibilities on a career website, job shadowing, learning how to study, or working through their resumé—something big happens. Perhaps they find their footing on a career pathway or become more comfortable in their own skin. Perhaps they recognize that there are many potential places in the work world for them or learn a strategy to help them cope with the things in life coming at them. You may not even know what the trigger is, but you know that someone who was languishing is now taking life on, seeing meaning in what they are doing, seeing clearly who they are, and feeling hopeful about their ability to handle the future.

You have probably seen this change to varying degrees in dozens, hundreds, or thousands of clients. In fact, you may have witnessed this kind of change so frequently that you take it for granted. "This is what I do," you say to yourself. "This is why I do this work. What's the big deal?" The big deal is that the career-related services you provide do far more than help people choose, prepare for, enter, and navigate career pathways—they change people's lives in ways that improve their mental health and overall wellbeing.

Your career development practice is a mental health intervention as well as a career development intervention. This is not a matter of choice, by the way: As a practitioner who does career development intervention—whether through counselling, teaching, advising, managing, or any other relevant function—you *will* influence mental health; you cannot avoid doing so. This may be a new and bold idea for many career development practitioners. If you are fearful or uncomfortable at the prospect of now having some responsibility for and influence on your

---

[1] "Client" is the term we will use to refer to anyone engaging with career development services, including students.

clients' mental health, then let us reassure you: This idea changes very little about the way career development practitioners go about doing their work. The changes are in how you understand that work and how you communicate the value of career development intervention and its role in supporting positive mental health.

Because you are reading this, we know you hold certain competencies in career development intervention and that these competencies have supported and created positive mental health outcomes for your clients. Our aims with this book are to help you learn enough about the connections between career development and mental health that you can confidently choose how you will

- be intentional about the mental health impact of your services,
- improve the mental health impact of your services,
- evaluate the mental health impact of your services, and
- communicate the mental health impact of your services to relevant stakeholders,

in complete alignment with the best available evidence and ethical guidelines, and within your boundaries of competence, your role, and the resources available to you.

Mental Health, Not Mental Illness

To achieve these aims, we must first and foremost disentangle the concepts of "mental illness" and "mental health." Everything we have described above applies to mental health, not mental illness. In this book:

- We do *not* argue that career development interventions are mental illness interventions (but we do explain their role in prevention).
- We do *not* claim that career development practitioners treat mental illness.
- We do *not* address strategies for helping individuals with mental illness manage their career development.

We delve into the distinctions between mental illness and mental health more deeply in the chapters ahead, and we differentiate other terms that often become blended. We raise this important distinction here because we want to be very clear about our intentions.

A Note for Practitioners Working with Individuals Affected by Mental Illness

If your primary clientele comprises individuals affected by mental illness, your practice includes specific concerns, methods, resources, and ethical considerations that will not be covered here. These considerations are thoroughly addressed in another CERIC-supported resource, *Career Services Guide: Supporting People Affected by Mental Health Issues*. Updated in 2018, *Career Services Guide* speaks to mental illness, employment and recovery, stigma, supports, workplace issues, legal concerns, and caring for the caregiver, among other important topics. Our book is an intentional complement to *Career Services Guide*. Although our book touches on some issues regarding mental illness, our primary focus is on mental health.

For more information and to download a copy of *Career Services Guide*, please visit www.ceric.ca/mentalhealth.

We have written this book primarily for those who see themselves as career development practitioners: those who help clients, one-on-one or in groups, with work readiness, career management/planning, educational planning, life transitions, work search, work maintenance, and/or career path advancement/management. This includes all of the following roles:

- Academic advisor
- Career advisor
- Career coach
- Career educator
- Career counsellor
- Employment advisor
- Employment counsellor
- Guidance counsellor
- Human resources practitioner
- Pre-retirement planner
- Vocational rehabilitation counsellor/practitioner

The ideas and practices in this book apply to youth in or out of formal schooling, adults in or out of the work world, and a wide range of settings and populations—from downtown centres for street youth to corporate headquarters with services for executives; from rural, isolated First Nations communities to densely populated urban centres; from services addressing very diverse populations to highly specialized services focused on a particular group or community (e.g., LGBTQ2S+, immigrants, refugees).

We also aim these ideas at two secondary (but only slightly so) audiences: supervisors/managers and academics/researchers. We expect the book to be of considerable value to the supervisors and managers of career development practitioners, particularly those responsible for service evaluation, fund development, community engagement/relationships, and service promotion/marketing. If you fit into this category and do not work directly with clients on the front lines, you may be most interested in the sections on evidence regarding work, career development, mental illness, and mental health relationships (Chapter 4); specific connections between career development interventions and mental health (Chapter 5); career development interventions and stress (Chapter 6); evaluation (Chapter 10); and communications (Chapter 11). Perceiving, understanding, improving, measuring, and communicating the mental health benefits of career development practice may be extremely important to your staff or organization, and are most certainly important to the field of career development generally.

We mentioned earlier the lack of sustained interest in the connections between career development and mental health, which we attribute in part to the overwhelming emphasis our funders and clients place on work/employment. Those who pay the bills for employment services, for example, are predominantly interested in employment, and this focus has shaped the ways we provide services and measure outcomes. Outcomes such as "improved mental health" or "increased capacity to deal with change" have not been priorities, particularly in terms of measuring results. The singular focus on employment as the single variable of interest has started to change in the past decade, at least in Canada, but the shift is slow. We hope this book and the work surrounding it will help accelerate research around the broader outcomes of career development services. This hope brings us to our next audience: researchers and academics.

Researchers and academics will find here what we believe to be a robust and testable model of career development and mental health relationships as well as descriptions of specific interventions to better achieve positive mental health outcomes within career development practice. We have made every effort to make career development– mental health connections based on the best available evidence and we have cited those sources. We welcome and encourage putting the ideas to the empirical test. In fact, one of our primary motives for doing this work on mental health is to stimulate research in this area. To this end, and as you will see in our review of the relevant and current evidence, there is quite a volume of research on career development and mental illness, but very little on career development and mental health. The field needs researchers to take this on, recognizing the astronomer Phil Plait's (2018) quote: "The price of doing science is admitting when you're wrong." Currently, the field of career development simply does not know the mental health effects of our work with any degree of certainty. It would be good to know, even if the results are not what we are hoping for.

Evidence, Not Proof

Regarding the research, a word of caution for all readers: We are trying to make a case that career development activities contribute to positive mental health. As our friend, colleague, and teacher Bryan Hiebert often reminded us, there is a difference between "evidence" and "proof." To ensure full disclosure, we want you to know that our case is built upon a great deal of evidence and far, far less proof. We have tried to be as transparent as possible about the strength of the evidence we bring forth (some of which is, admittedly, circumstantial). We invite readers to be wary, and to question and reflect on the ideas we present. Our field has a long way to go to convincingly demonstrate the links we highlight in this book. There is work to be done to develop our profession. If we can effectively make the case for career development's role in mental health, there is potential for our profession to make even greater positive impacts in our communities and the lives of our clients.

After Reading This Book, You Will...

- Understand the distinctions between mental health and mental illness
- Be more aware of how mental health concerns manifest themselves in career development practice
- Better understand the relationship between career development and mental health
- Recognize a range of career development strategies that support positive mental health
- Better understand the career development processes and mechanisms that explain how work (or meaningful career direction) addresses fundamental psychological needs and how its absence can lead to distress
- Understand ethical principles for career development practitioners related to mental health/illness issues and the boundaries of competence
- More effectively refer to and/or work collaboratively with mental health/mental illness professionals

- Be able to use specific strategies to bolster mental health via career development practice
- Have tools to evaluate the mental health impact of your career development services
- Have a strategy for communicating the mental health impact of your career development services to key stakeholders

About the Book

This book becomes increasingly practical chapter by chapter. We move (effortlessly, we hope!) from an overall rationale for connecting career development and mental health all the way through to a step-by-step description of how to communicate your practice's successful mental health outcomes. In between, we describe and discuss important concepts and definitions, existing research, models that could guide practice, methods for ethically using strategies and skills to incorporate mental health in your practice, and tools/instructions for evaluating outcomes.

We intend for readers to read all the chapters and do so in sequence. We know enough about human behaviour, however, to accept that you might read non-sequentially or may simply want to get to the parts that are practical. If you are time-crunched and/or practice-oriented, we hope the following descriptions help you make effective and efficient decisions about how you use the book.

Chapters 2 and 3 establish the need to connect mental health and career development and the core concepts/terminology that have an enormous impact on how these connections are understood and communicated.

Chapter 3 Is Crucial

We urge you not to skip Chapter 3 and to read it before you read subsequent chapters. Chapter 3 addresses fundamental distinctions, in particular the distinction between mental health and mental illness, that are pivotal to our case and purpose. Much of the remainder of the book may be somewhat confusing if you see these as the ends of a single continuum. At the very least, read the description of Corey Keyes's dual continua model of wellbeing.

Chapter 4 describes the research regarding the relationships among career development, work, mental health, and mental illness. This will be of considerable value to you if you need to be convinced—or you want to convince others—that career development and mental health are connected. From a practical standpoint, you want to find enough in this chapter to be able to look clients in the eye and unapologetically say, "I am a career development practitioner/educator, not a mental health professional, but I know the research clearly shows that career-related concerns are related to mental health concerns."

Chapter 5 provides a model that attempts to illustrate how career development intervention produces five sets of effects or outcomes that are related to mental health outcomes. You will readily identify the outcomes of your particular career development practice by quickly scanning this chapter, and then you can zero in on the description of these outcomes.

You really cannot get by without reading **Chapter 6** because it lays out the common denominator of all career development intervention vis-à-vis mental health: stress and coping. The description of the relationship between career development intervention and stress/coping concepts is oddly practical. We are very sure that reading this conceptual chapter will give you ideas for your practice.

Chapters 7–9 are all "how-to" chapters: how to incorporate mental health into your practice ethically, how to do so practically, and how to use skills you already possess in ways that intentionally bolster mental health, respectively. These are the go-to chapters for readers most interested in practice and practicality.

But wait, there's even more practical content! **Chapters 10 and 11** are practical in a different way—they are "how-to and then do." These chapters walk you through the processes of gathering evidence regarding the mental health outcomes of your practice (Chapter 10) so that you have what you need to communicate effectively to stakeholders (Chapter 11). "There is nothing so practical as reliable and adequate funding" is our corollary to Lewin's maxim that "There is nothing so practical as a good theory" (Lewin, 1943). These two chapters provide step-by-step methods by which you can assure yourself that your career development interventions lead to mental health outcomes while gathering evidence of how to do so even more effectively, and then convincingly communicating this effectiveness to clients, administrators, allied professionals, and, of course, funders.

Chapter 12 is our rousing conclusion and call to action. It is not practical, but it is brief!

Much of this book is devoted to the importance of connecting career development and mental health. For now, we leave you with one important reason for doing so: Career development concerns and mental health issues cannot be treated as mutually exclusive. Each client who comes to you with their career-related concerns is a whole person. "Seeing" and working with the whole person—viewing career planning as life-planning and career development intervention as life intervention—can only strengthen your practice and its outcomes.

A Request

Thank you for investing your time and energy in reading this book. We hope it will be relevant and useful to career development practitioners and their stakeholders, and we would like to make it more useful in future iterations. This part does not help you directly, but it will make a big difference to future readers. We invite you to complete a short evaluation of the book. In return, we will do our very best to (1) create a better second edition of the book and (2) incorporate your feedback in other career development and mental health resources (e.g., workshops, webinars) we are working on.

To complete the evaluation, go to www.life-role.com/CDMH.htm.

Thank you in advance!

Work is at once so commonplace that it is studied by few scholars and so familiar that practical [people] tend to believe its problems can be handled by common-sense methods.

Donald Super

To Ponder...
Think of your social circle: family members, friends, neighbours, colleagues, and acquaintances. Picture those you know who live with mental illness. What percentage of your group do they represent? How many others in your group do you think may be on the edge of experiencing mental health problems or symptoms of mental illness?

2. Why Connect Career Development and Mental Health?

Mental health/illness concerns and substance use disorders affect at least 15% of the world's population, or 1.1 billion people (Ritchie & Roser, 2019). To put this in perspective, this is the sum of the populations of Australia, Canada, France, Germany, Italy, Japan, New Zealand, the Philippines, Russia, Spain, the United Kingdom, and the United States (Index Mundi, 2019). At least 4% of the world's population experience depression and 4% are affected by anxiety disorders (World Health Organization, 2017). We use the term "at least" because mental health/illness disorders are under-reported, especially in cultures and countries in which it is taboo to discuss or admit to mental health problems. In countries making efforts to tackle the stigma associated with mental illness, these percentages are higher. In Canada and Australia, for example, the ratio 1 in 5 (20%) (Mental Health Commission of Canada [MHCC], 2011; Australian Bureau of Statistics [ABS], 2007) is commonly used to express the proportion of the population likely to experience a mental illness or mental health problem within a given year. Estimates of the number of individuals who will experience a mental illness in their lifetime range from 1 in 2 (MHCC, 2011) to 1 in 3 (Pearson, Janz, & Ali, 2013).

The social, emotional, and economic costs of mental health disorders and mental illness are high. Mental illness is currently the most expensive disability in workplaces. For example, in any given week, at least 500,000 Canadians take sick days due to a mental illness (Dewa, Chau, & Dermer, 2010). Mental disorders in youth are the second-highest expenditure in Canada's hospital care (Mental Health Commission of Canada, 2013) and the highest in Australia in 2016–17 (Australian Institute for Health and Welfare, 2018). Suicide accounts for about a quarter of all deaths among those aged 15–24 within Canada (this is the third-highest rate in the industrialized world) (Statistics Canada, 2018). Among those aged 15–24 in Australia, suicide is the leading cause of death (Australian Bureau of Statistics, 2017). Globally, suicide is the second leading cause of death for those aged 15–29 (World Health Organization, 2019a).

There are hosts of troubling statistics regarding the incidence and costs of mental health/illness problems, but these numbers barely scratch the surface in revealing the social and emotional costs. It is one thing to count the number of work days lost to mental health issues or mental illness; it is another to reckon the emotional impact on the people experiencing an issue or illness: explaining their absence to co-workers or bosses, worrying about how they will be perceived if they admit to experiencing mental health issues, feeling guilty for increasing the workload of their colleagues by being away, perceiving themselves as somehow "lesser" than others, and explaining to their children and/or partner why they did not go to work.

Fortunately, there has been a great wave of interest in mental health and illness in recent years. This interest seems to be reducing the stigma surrounding mental health/illness issues, particularly in the Western world, and enabling open discussions about ways to grapple with them. Governments, not-for-profits, and corporations are devoting significant resources to awareness-raising, research, and programming. The following is a small sample of such resources in Australia and Canada (Dollar values are in referenced country's currency.):

- Through the Bell Let's Talk campaign, Bell has committed over $100 million to mental health initiatives in Canada since 2010 (bell.ca/letstalk).

- Australia's 2019 budget boosted funding for youth mental health by $461 million (https://www.health.gov.au/resources/publications/budget-2019-20-prioritising-mental-health-youth-mental-health-and-suicide-prevention-plan).

- Australia's 2019 budget also allocated an additional $275 million to support a range of national and local mental health initiatives (https://www.health.gov.au/resources/publications/budget-2019-20-prioritising-mental-health-community-mental-health).

- The RBC Youth Mental Well-being Project has contributed more than $34 million to Canadian organizations working with youth and family mental health concerns (https://www.rbc.com/community-social-impact/youth/index.html).

- In 2017, the Canadian government allocated $5 billion over 10 years to improve access to mental health services (https://www.canada.ca/en/health-canada/news/2017/04/minister_philpotthighlightssignificantinvestmentsforbetteraccess.html).

- The Mental Health Commission of Canada received about $14 million in grant funding from the federal government in 2018 (https://www.mentalhealthcommission.ca/sites/default/files/Mental%252520Health%252520Commission%252520Of%252520Canada_PreBudget%252520Submission_EN_1_0.pdf).

- The Canadian Mental Health Association national office's revenues for 2016–2017 were over $1.5 million; divisional offices have additional revenues (https://cmha.ca/wp-content/uploads/2017/09/annualreport-2016-17_EN_FINAL.pdf).

According to the Centre for Addiction and Mental Health (CAMH), the economic burden of mental illness and mental health problems in Canada is approximately $51 billion annually (CAMH, 2019) and the estimate for the same figure in Australia is $60 billion annually (Australian Government National Mental Health Commission, 2016). Globally, losses due to mental disorders are estimated to amount to US$16 trillion between 2010 and 2030 (Bloom et al., 2011). The enormity of this figure is attributed both to early age of onset of mental health concerns and loss of productivity over the lifespan. So, it makes sense to see so much funding devoted to doing something about these problems. And while we fully endorse committing significant resources to mental health/illness initiatives, we have two main concerns regarding the allocation of these resources. Both concerns are influenced by our vested interests as career development practitioners, and we will be perfectly clear about those interests below.

Addressing Symptoms at the Expense of Causes

Our first worry is that the great interest in mental health/illness has pitted and may continue to pit "mental health" against "career development." Consider policy-makers, funders, and organizational administrators reviewing their finite budgets and having to make decisions about where to allocate resources. The human resources department in a corporation, for example, might decide to devote a portion of its budget to stress management workshops, mental health awareness, or mindfulness tools for employees. These initiatives may well be effective, but if the decision to pursue them is made at the expense of supporting the core career development needs of employees, the HR department may do the organization and its employees a great disservice. By reducing support for career development in favour of funding targeted mental health initiatives, the HR department may inadvertently increase the likelihood of negative mental health outcomes resulting from issues such as poor employee-role "fit," inappropriate workload demands, or career path blockages. The *symptoms* of some of these issues (e.g., anxiety, disengagement, stress) may be alleviated by mental health initiatives, but their *causes* will not be addressed if services that get to the root of problems are removed, reduced, or absent altogether.

As we articulate in subsequent chapters, career development interventions and processes strengthen mental health and can create protective factors against mental illness. Choosing "mental health" over "career development" in a community, organization, school, or post-secondary institution may help administrators show they are doing something about mental health, but choices that make for good optics may perpetuate the problem.

Think about it this way: If a hospital administrator was faced with an unsanitary water supply and limited resources, would the administrator choose to fund antibiotics over clean water? Both contribute to health/illness and both cost money. Antibiotics may help cure the problems caused by dirty water, but dealing with the dirty water certainly cannot be abandoned if there is to be any hope of lowering the antibiotics budget. Luckily, in this case and many others, the choice is obvious and the need for balanced funding is reasonably easy to see. In the case of "mental health" versus "career development," the choice is perhaps less clear, particularly to those outside the career development profession. Career development interventions can result in a broad range of career development outcomes, including significant personal, social, economic, and work-related changes. Employment outcomes are vitally important, and though they are one type of outcome—the tip of the iceberg really—it is the one our field has measured, and measured well, because our livelihood as a profession has depended on it. Our field has not made the case that career development interventions are mental health protective factors. Administrators cannot be blamed for choosing "mental health" over "career development": We have not provided evidence of the connections between the two.

Missed Opportunities

Our second concern about the allocation of mental health/illness resources is one of missed opportunities. Career development is not a field flooded with research funds. Very few Australian or Canadian universities teach career development at the undergraduate level (the province of Quebec's institutions being the enviable exception) and only slightly more have faculty who conduct research in the area of career development (again, Quebec being the exception). There are currently no master's degree or PhD programs in career development in Canada outside of Quebec (though career counselling courses are offered in some counselling programs) and few post-graduate programs in Australia.

Our field's history is limited, and our collective research base and infrastructure are weak. We need to seek and take advantage of all available research opportunities. The current interest in mental health may provide such opportunities, which we could use to engage in the conceptualization and research needed to determine

- that career development interventions can result in positive mental health outcomes;

- how, specifically, career development interventions influence mental health;

- how, specifically, career development interventions that influence mental health can do so even more effectively and efficiently; and

- how additional or new career development interventions could simultaneously achieve strong career development and positive mental health outcomes.

If we could determine the above, we would first and foremost be able to clearly articulate the case for career development as a mental health intervention and bypass the "career development versus mental health" funding debate. Over time, public and stakeholder understanding of our work as a wellbeing intervention would stabilize the funding for our services. Second, we could get better at what we do, and potentially *much* better. We all know that we contribute to mental health and wellbeing, but we understand our impact there to be a by-product of creating career-related outcomes. If we did our work with great career development *and* solid mental health outcomes in mind, we believe that both sets of outcomes would improve. Quite simply, career development practice will improve when we understand, study, and measure its broader impact on mental health outcomes—outcomes that extend beyond a resumé, a job, a career plan, a self-portrait, or whatever else our services help our clients to achieve. We need to show that, in addition to all of these tangible outcomes, career development can help clients to develop greater resilience and coping resources, thereby bolstering their capacity for maintaining positive mental health.

Summary

Mental health has captured the public's attention as an important issue and goal. The career development field has not made the case that career development interventions affect mental health, nor has it shown how and to what degree they do so. The field needs to uncover this evidence where it exists and seek evidence where it does not. Otherwise, attention, energy, and resources may be diverted away from career development efforts to more overt mental health initiatives, simultaneously undermining the fundamentals of clients' mental health as well as degrading the service capacity of career development.

Reflection Questions

1. How might people in your life with mental illness or mental health concerns benefit from effective career development intervention?

2. How would knowing more about the connections between career development and mental health benefit you in your work?

3. What concerns you the most when you think about connecting career development and mental health in your practice? What would you need to learn to reduce this concern?

Words are, in my not-so-humble opinion, our most inexhaustible source of magic.

Professor Dumbledore (J.K. Rowling)

To Ponder...

Think of a time when a neighbour, colleague, or acquaintance used a career-related term inappropriately. What did you do?

3. Let's Be Clear: Disentangling Tangled Terms

Words may well be an inexhaustible source of magic, but they are also an inexhaustible source of confusion, misunderstandings, and false assumptions. You may remember learning the concept of "mass" in science class and immediately translating this into the word "weight" in your head. Your teacher undoubtedly spent much time trying to break you and your classmates of this mental equivalence, but we suspect that to this day you still think "weight" when someone says "mass." There are many examples of technical terms that have a different, less-accurate meaning in everyday use or terms that are falsely equated. For example, most people hear

- "negative reinforcement" and think "punishment,"
- "self-efficacy" and think "self-esteem,"
- "velocity" and think "speed,"
- "facial tissue" and think "Kleenex®" (which must really irritate the Scott® tissue people over at Kimberly-Clark),
- "career" and think "doctor" or "lawyer,"
- "mental health" and think "mental illness," or
- "career development" and think "work."

In most cases, such synonymizing is not problematic; either the context determines exactly what is meant or there is a common understanding of what is meant among the people communicating with each other. When the meanings of distinct terms are blended, however, confusion can arise. Ask a career development practitioner what "career" means, and "doctor" and "lawyer" do not even come up in the conversation, except perhaps as examples of the tens of thousands of occupations available to individuals.

For our purposes, there are two pairs of concepts whose definitions must be clarified: mental health/mental illness and career development/work. We begin disentangling these below.

Career Development and Work

Career Development

Here are two definitions of career development adopted by career development practitioners in Australia and Canada, respectively:

> Career development is the process of managing life, learning and work over the lifespan. (Career Education Assocation of Victoria, 2019)

> Career development is the lifelong process of managing learning, work, leisure, and transitions in order to move toward a personally determined and evolving preferred future. (Canadian Standards and Guidelines for Career Development Practitioners [CSGCDP], 2012, p. 2)

"Work" is an important part of each definition and the main reason clients approach career development practitioners. However, work is only a part of the definitions and, in the long run, not the most important part. The verb "managing" is key—it is the action that we need to help clients with now and in the future. Practitioners cannot manage their clients, so living up to these definitions means *helping clients learn how to manage themselves*. With the ability to manage, clients will be able to handle work-related issues on their own (or with occasional help from practitioners) but will also be able to deal with other life issues.

The distinction between career development and work is important because career development practice can greatly contribute to an individual's ability to manage regardless of whether or not they choose an occupational destination or career path and find work (paid or unpaid). Career development interventions have effects on individuals that are independent of the outcome of finding work.

The above definitions of career development were developed by bodies that represent practitioners in the field. There are a variety of scholarly and theoretical conceptions of career development, but you may be surprised by how few theories explicitly define "career development." For theorists of career development, it seems their theories *are* their definitions of career development. For example, we are not sure you will find any sentence written by Donald Super, the pre-eminent proponent of career development as a concept, that begins "Career development is..." Theories of career development typically view career development as a general subset of human development—a subset with a particular focus on the individual's relationship with work over the lifespan. We have used practitioner-based definitions here to highlight what most career development theorists agree upon: *One's relationship with work is a changing process, not an event.* The degree to which individuals can manage that process, and the ways in which they should attempt to manage it, are less agreed-upon in career development theory.

Work

Physicists aside,[2] most people think of work as a set of activities one does for remuneration. This common, nontechnical definition is reasonably close to how Canadian and Australian career development practitioners define work:

> Work is a set of activities with an intended set of outcomes, from which it is hoped that a person will derive personal satisfaction and contribute to some greater goal. Work is not necessarily tied to paid employment, but to meaningful and satisfying activities (e.g., volunteer work, hobbies). (CSGCDP, 2012, p. 4)

---

[2] In physics, work is the product of the force moving an object and the distance it moves.

A set of activities such as paid employment, parenting, care work, or volunteering from which it is hoped a person will derive personal satisfaction. (Career Industry Council of Australia, 2019, p. 31)

In this book, we will mostly treat work as a role one performs for an employer for pay. We do so simply because the research in the area of work and mental illness and mental health, done by economists, medical practitioners, psychologists, sociologists, and others, uses the general public's connotation of work as "employment" or "paid set of activities."

Mental Illness and Mental Health

Traditionally, mental health and mental illness have been viewed as two states at either end of a single continuum: More mental health implies less mental illness, and more mental illness means less mental health. However, when we look at definitions of mental illness and mental health, we see details and a qualifier that challenge this view.

Mental Illness

As we did with definitions of career development, let's consider three field-based definitions of mental illness:

> ...[a] mental illness is a clinically diagnosable disorder that significantly interferes with an individual's cognitive, emotional or social abilities. (Australian Government Department of Health, 2008)

> Mental illnesses are characterized by alterations in thinking, mood or behaviour associated with significant distress and impaired functioning. (Public Health Agency of Canada, 2015)

> Mental disorders comprise a broad range of problems, with different symptoms. However, they are generally characterized by some combination of abnormal thoughts, emotions, behaviour, and relationships with others. Examples are schizophrenia, depression, intellectual disabilities, and disorders

due to drug abuse. Most of these disorders can be successfully treated. (World Health Organization, 2018)

The Government of Canada uses a definition that is somewhat broader than that of Australia (which requires a clinical diagnosis), but all three emphasize abnormal or altered thought, behaviour, and mood that impede the individual's functioning. Scholarly or theoretical approaches to mental illness are complex. They range from the non-existence of mental illness or the view that it is created, understood, and perpetuated by the language used to describe it (see, for example, Szasz, 1974, and Hillman, 1975) to the detailed diagnostic criteria of the American Psychiatric Association's *Diagnostic and Statistical Manual of Mental Disorders (DSM-5)* (American Psychiatric Association, 2013). The DSM-5 is a diagnostic system that, at its best, allows professionals to meaningfully explore client concerns in a way that leads to successful intervention. Further, it ought to give us a shared meaning about the concerns our clients are facing and thus help us to share information about those concerns more effectively. However, one criticism of the DSM-5 is its overemphasis on biological factors and limited consideration of psychosocial and contextual factors (Raskin, 2018). Using the system entails understanding mental illness as a biological or brain problem rather than as something that might result from the stressors or circumstances one is facing. Despite the criticism, the DSM-5 is still a standard and will likely play a role in determining how we, our clients, and other professionals think about and intervene with mental illness conditions and mental health concerns. As we noted earlier, our primary focus here is on career development intervention as support for positive mental health.

Mental Health

The Australian government, the Canadian government, and the World Health Organization define mental health, explicitly or implicitly, in positive ways rather than as the absence of mental illness:

> Mental health is not simply the absence of mental illness.... [A] state of emotional and social wellbeing in which the individual can cope with the normal stresses of life and achieve his or her potential. (Australian Government Department of Health and Ageing, 2003)

the capacity of each and all of us to feel, think, act in ways that enhance our ability to enjoy life and deal with the challenges we face. It is a positive sense of emotional and spiritual well-being that respects the importance of culture, equity, social justice, interconnections and personal dignity. (Public Health Agency of Canada, 2014)

Mental health is defined as a state of well-being in which every individual realizes his or her own potential, can cope with the normal stresses of life, can work productively and fruitfully, and is able to make a contribution to her or his community. (World Health Organization, 2019b)

At the core of each definition are the concepts of wellbeing, managing stress/challenges, productive contributions to society, and fulfilment of one's potential.

Below, we do what we avoided doing with definitions of career development, work, and mental illness: We take a more detailed look at theoretical and scholarly approaches to conceptualizing mental health. We do so because, as you will see, the nuances of mental health are pivotal to our overall case that career development intervention has a positive mental health impact. Understanding the details of mental health will also inform how we, as a field, choose to measure the mental health outcomes of our work. Our deep dive into mental health concepts begins with the work of Corey Keyes.

Corey Keyes's Dual Continua Model: A Different Way of Defining Mental Illness and Mental Health

In the mid-1990s, Corey Keyes, an American sociologist and psychologist, posited that mental health co-exists with mental illness, and strong mental health (flourishing) may help mitigate the effects of mental illness. In his dual continua model of mental illness and mental health, high/low mental health is one continuum and high/low mental illness is the other (see Figure 3.1). There is a solid rationale for distinguishing mental health and mental illness as well as considerable evidence for the existence of Keyes's two continua (Keyes, 2005; see also Keyes, 2006; Keyes et al., 2008; Keyes, 2014).

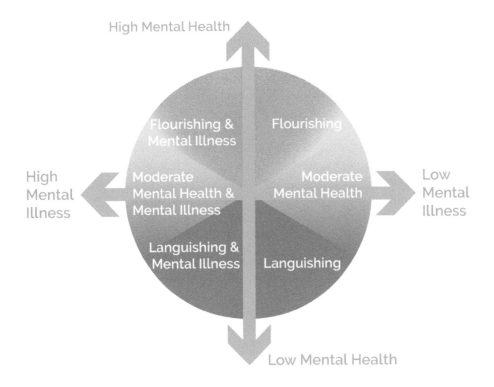

Figure 3.1. **Keyes's Dual Continua Model of Mental Health.** Adapted from Keyes, C. L. M. (2014). Mental health as a complete state: How the salutogenic perspective completes the picture. In G.F. Bauer & O. Hammig (Eds.), *Bridging occupational, organizational and public health: A transdisciplinary approach.* New York: Springer, p. 182.

Keyes's model may require a real shift in thinking for you. It certainly did for us. The model proposes that someone can have a diagnosed mental illness and simultaneously be mentally healthy, and this is not a mainstream view. Western society typically understands these as states on a single continuum: One either has a mental illness or is mentally healthy. And yet, viewing mental illness and mental health according to Keyes's model is similar to the way we think about physical health: A person can have a physical condition or disease and yet be in good physical health. For example, one can have diabetes and yet be very physically healthy.

We suspect you can immediately bring to mind friends, family, or clients who struggle with mental illness yet also give every indication of being mentally healthy. A long-time friend and colleague of Dave's, whom we will call Mariam, lives fully in all her life roles and important relationships. Her full-time work with youth, active and frequent pursuits in nature, volunteer work with animals, commitment to her significant other, travel experiences, and ongoing strong relationships with friends keep her busy and fulfilled. Since adolescence, Mariam has experienced deep and painful bouts of depression. She manages the various demands of her life well, contributes to society through meaningful work, develops and maintains strong friendships, and is generally upbeat, warm, unselfconscious, and full of humour. Those who meet her in work or social settings would not have an inkling that she has experiences with mental illness and has benefitted greatly from anti-anxiety and anti-depressant medications. In fact, they might see her as an exemplar of mental health.

Those who know Mariam beyond casual work and social interactions occasionally see, usually indirectly, a person who needs to be more careful than most about managing activities so that she does not become overwhelmed. They also see that she can fall into a dark place of depression where she closes herself off, stays alone, and keeps away from the world. Mariam's mental health, however, enables her to communicate what she is doing and why, accept her symptoms (rather than using valuable energy fighting them), do what she needs to do, and then pull out of dark episodes more quickly than she would otherwise. Her mental health, which she actively works on, has lowered the frequency of her depressive episodes and bolstered her capacity to advocate on her own behalf for accommodations that enable her to function well at and outside of work.

As will become apparent in the coming pages, the dual continua model is a very helpful framework for career development practitioners. Career development theorists have claimed (or assumed) for several decades now that career development contributes to positive mental health, but the field has been reluctant to argue that career development intervention is an intervention for mental illness. With Keyes's model, our field may have a way to meaningfully discuss our collective contribution to mental health without risking false claims of "treating" mental illness. Furthermore, if there is evidence that strong mental health (flourishing) helps individuals better manage their mental illness and/or mitigate the illness's effects, we will be able to show that career development intervention is an important, if indirect, contributor to mitigating mental illness concerns.

The Components of Mental Health

For Keyes, mental health comprises three kinds of wellbeing: emotional (pleasurable feelings), social (fitting in a group), and psychological (developing as a person).[3] Each of these characteristics is described below.

Emotional Wellbeing

Emotional wellbeing can be roughly equated with happiness. It includes positive feelings about one's self as well as overall life satisfaction. The definitions of mental illness provided above include the idea of distress and those of mental health describe or imply enjoyment. Feeling happy or satisfied seems a natural, and perhaps obvious, part of a mental health definition. A quick glance at the self-help section of a bookstore will reveal many titles that include the word "happiness," lending further support to the idea that feeling good is part of mental health. Happiness researcher Shawn Achor (2010), physician Deepak Chopra (2009), Buddhist spiritual leader Thich Nhat Hanh (2005), Anglican theologian Desmond Tutu and the spiritual leader of Tibet, the Dalai Lama (Dalai Lama, Tutu, & Abrams, 2016) are among the many self-help and spiritual guides who have published books with "happiness" in the title.

For our purposes as career development practitioners, the inclusion of emotional wellbeing in mental health makes sense. However, if you are asking yourself whether or not mentally healthy individuals are always happy (or should be), you are not alone. Galderisi, Heinz, Kastrup, Beezhold, and Sartorius (2015) pondered the same question:

> In fact, regarding well-being as a key aspect of mental health is difficult to reconcile with the many challenging life situations in which well-being may even be unhealthy: most people would consider as mentally unhealthy an individual experiencing a state of well-being while killing several persons during a war action, and would regard as healthy

---

[3] Keyes uses the language of ancient Greek philosophers to distinguish hedonic, or pleasure-oriented, wellbeing and eudamonic wellbeing, or wellbeing with respect to virtue (living up to one's potential or exceptional functioning). Eudamonic wellbeing is composed of social wellbeing and psychological wellbeing.

a person feeling desperate after being fired from his/her job in a situation in which occupational opportunities are scarce. (p. 231)

We raise this counterpoint to emotional wellbeing as a component of mental health to acknowledge the complexity of concepts of mental health and wellbeing and their cultural interpretations. What seems obvious at first glance may actually be dead wrong or only partially correct; what seems completely counterintuitive may be the thing that works best, depending on context. With this caveat in mind, we tentatively accept that most of the time and in most contexts, emotional wellbeing is an important component of mental health. We also recognize that feeling good cannot be the only possible indicator of mental health; it does not take much reflection to think of individuals who are not mentally healthy but feel happy.

Psychological Wellbeing

Keyes's conception of the psychological aspects of mental health relies heavily on the work of Ryff (1989) and others who have described six domains of psychological wellbeing. These domains were derived from theories of human development, conceptions of ideal functioning, and approaches to mental health, and each contributes to the ability of individuals to make full use of their characteristics, or to "become all they can be" to paraphrase Abraham Maslow. We quote Westerhof and Keyes's (2010) synopsis of these domains directly:

1. *Self-acceptance:* a positive and acceptant attitude toward aspects of self in past and present;
2. *Purpose in life:* goals and beliefs that affirm a sense of direction and meaning in life;
3. *Autonomy:* self-direction as guided by one's own socially accepted internal standards;
4. *Positive relations with others:* having satisfying personal relationships in which empathy and intimacy are expressed;
5. *Environmental mastery:* the capability to manage the complex environment according to one's own needs;
6. *Personal growth:* the insight into one's own potential for self-development. (p. 111)

As a career development practitioner, this list probably resonates with you as aims you and your clients have for your work together.

Social Wellbeing

The sociocultural element of wellbeing includes ideas such as belonging, responsibility, being valued, and relationships. Keyes included social components of wellbeing, derived from the work of sociologists and social psychologists, in his explanation of mental health in recognition of the fact that humans live in social groups. Again, we quote Westerhof and Keyes directly to describe the dimensions of social wellbeing:

1. *Social coherence:* being able to make meaning of what is happening in society;
2. *Social acceptance:* a positive attitude toward others while acknowledging their difficulties;
3. *Social actualization:* the belief that the community has potential and can evolve positively;
4. *Social contribution:* the feeling that one's activities contribute to and are valued by society;
5. *Social integration:* a sense of belonging to a community. (p. 111)

Reviewing this list from the perspective of career development, do you see ways in which your work is intimately involved with each of these dimensions?

For Keyes, these three kinds of wellbeing fully elaborate the characteristics of mental health in the World Health Organization's definition. We repeat the WHO's definition below, with the three kinds of wellbeing inserted alongside the roughly corresponding descriptions:

> Mental health is defined as a state of well-being [emotional wellbeing] in which every individual realizes his or her own potential, can cope with the normal stresses of life [psychological wellbeing], can work productively and fruitfully, and is able to make a contribution to her or his community [social wellbeing].

We will further explore the definitions and characteristics of mental health in Chapter 4, when we present a model to link career development effects to mental health, and in Chapter 10, when we consider how to measure outcomes and impact.

One More Distinction: The Career Development Practitioner Is Not a Mental Health Professional

From an ethical perspective, it is important to distinguish between mental health clinicians, such as clinical social workers, psychologists, and psychiatrists, and career development practitioners. There can certainly be an overlap in subject matter, as when a clinical social worker discusses career development concerns, or a career development specialist provides health and wellness strategies and makes a referral to a mental health professional for counselling (e.g., when a client presents with concerns about anxiety, depression, or suicide). In the latter instance, it is necessary for practitioners in their respective fields to collaborate in order to provide the best care. In the same instance, a career development practitioner would also be well advised to have suicide prevention training and relevant resources at hand, should the topic of suicide arise. Although it is not a requirement, it is beneficial for career development programs to include a mental health professional on their team.

We raise the distinction and overlap between career development practitioners and mental health professionals (knowing that some people, such as Michael, can be both) because we want to be very clear that we do not intend for career development practitioners to be seen as mental health professionals. We will argue—and show—that the work of all career development practitioners contributes to mental health, but we do not want that sentiment conflated with the thought that career development practitioners are mental health professionals. They are not. Nonetheless, it is clear that psychological intervention, even when provided by a mental health professional, can vary in its effectiveness at addressing mental health concerns (Duncan, Miller, Wampold, & Hubble, 2010). Other important relationships (consider the importance of supportive friendships, familial and work relationships) can also do much to contribute to positive mental health. Mental health is a shared responsibility for us all, whether in a work role or functioning as a whole human being in other parts of life.

Summary

Two linguistic and conceptual distinctions are pivotal to connecting career development and mental health. The first is between "mental health" and "mental illness," which have traditionally been viewed as states on a single continuum but which Corey Keyes (Westerhof & Keyes, 2010) places on two intersecting continua. His model makes it clear that a person can be mentally healthy (flourishing) while having a mental illness and that a person can be mentally unhealthy (languishing) but not have a mental illness. The work of career development practitioners can contribute to flourishing or mental health but does not directly address mental illness.

The second key distinction is between "career development," which is a process of managing learning, work, and life, and "work," which is one possible outcome of career development. It is well-known that work contributes to mental health; we now need to show that career development does, too.

Reflection Questions

1. If you were to plot your position on Keyes's dual continua model, where are you generally?

2. How have you typically conceptualized mental health and mental illness in your workplace? Does the information in this chapter change this conceptualization, and if so, how?

3. Ponder your main sources of information regarding mental illness and mental health. What new sources might you want to seek out and consult, and why? In what areas might you want to round out these sources?

As always in life, people want a simple answer...
and it's always wrong.

Susan Greenfield

To Ponder...

Think of a time at work when you felt your mental health
was really taxed. Now, think of a time at work in which
your mental health was bolstered. What were the key
differences between the two situations?

4. The Latest Research

Research regarding the relationship between career development
and mental health suffers from the terminological confusions and
conflations we described in the previous chapter. For example, the
traditional conception of a single mental health-illness continuum has
resulted in a great deal of research on "mental health" that is really
about the presence or absence of mental illness. On the whole, the
research has not kept up with conceptual shifts in either mental health
or career development. Recognizing these difficulties, we do our best
in this chapter to lay out the evidence for the relationships among four
sets of variables illustrated in Figure 4.1: mental illness, mental health,
career development, and work. We differentiated mental health and
mental illness as well as career development and work in Chapter 3.
Here, we provide a synopsis of the bidirectional relationships between
mental illness and work, mental illness and career development, mental
health and work, and mental health and career development.

The core information in this chapter is from "The broader aims of career development: Mental
health, wellbeing and work," by D. E. Redekopp and M. Huston, 2018, *British Journal of Guidance
and Counselling, 47*(2), pp. 246–257.

Figure 4.1. **The relationships among mental illness, mental health, career development, and work.**

You may question our decision to review mental illness studies in a book focusing on mental health. You may also wonder why we summarize research on work in a book about career development. We question the inclusion of these areas, too. We would really like to home in on the crux of the matter and answer the question, "How does career development influence mental health"? The reality is that these constructs are intertwined

- conceptually (even if mental illness and mental health are distinct, for example, we know they are related),
- historically (in the grand scheme of things, the dual continua model is quite recent),

- socially/culturally (no matter what theory says, stakeholders such as funders and clients will have their own take on these concepts), and
- practically (there is far more research on work and mental illness than on career development and mental health; it would be a brief review indeed if it addressed only career development and mental health!).

As a field, we need to understand all these connections in order to adequately contextualize any of them for ourselves, our funders, and our clients.

We present below our research summaries starting with mental illness and work relationships and then proceed, pair by pair, through the various combinations, culminating with career development's relationships with mental health. We provide less detail on the mental illness connections, recognizing that this research has been summarized in *Career Services Guide: Supporting People Affected by Mental Health Issues*, a CERIC-supported publication highlighted in Chapter 1. We connect the research base to the realities of front-line career development practice via anecdotes and examples provided by career development practitioners in Canada and Australia.[4]

Spoiler alert: Teasing apart conceptions of mental illness and mental health as well as career development and work reveals important gaps in the evidence!

---

[4] The online surveys were completed prior to the delivery of sessions in Canada and Australia on career development and mental health connections for career development practitioners. Practitioners were asked (1) to use pseudonyms rather than clients' real names, (2) if they wanted their name acknowledged, and (3) for permission to use their responses in resources we might develop on this topic.

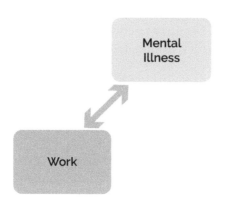

The Impact of Mental Illness on Work

There is a great deal of research on the effects of mental illness with regards to seeking, finding, and keeping work but there is still much we do not know and much research to be done.

"Mental illness" is a very broad category that includes well over 100 disorders (American Psychiatric Association, 2013), some of which may have little impact on work (e.g., phobias) and some that can, in some circumstances, have catastrophic consequences for engaging in the workforce (e.g., schizophrenia). Also, mental illness falls along a continuum of severity, with minor and sporadic mental illness concerns having less of an impact than major and chronic concerns.[5] Finally, mental illness may be undiagnosed even though present and affecting work. In some instances, neither research studies nor research reviews are entirely clear about the type of mental illness in question, its severity, or whether the illness is diagnosed, self-reported, or both.

With the above qualifiers in mind, here are some highlights of the evidence regarding the impact of mental illness on work:

- Mental illness is the leading cause of both work absence due to sickness and long-term disability (Petrie et al., 2018).

---

[5] Unless otherwise stated, any references to types of mental illness are derived from the American Psychiatric Association's *Diagnostic and Statistical Manual of Mental Disorders (DSM–5)*.

- Severe and permanent mental illness can prevent entry into, and participation in, working life (Waddell & Burton, 2006).
- Anxiety, depression, and substance use disorders are the most common mental illness concerns that interfere with working life (Harvey et al., 2013; Joyce et al., 2016).
- Costs of mental illness result from
  - absenteeism (due to increased sickness, poor health, physical maladies such as back pain),
  - presenteeism (working while incapacitated due to illness),
  - poor work performance (reduced productivity, accidents, impaired decision-making),
  - poor attitude (low motivation and commitment, ineffectiveness, poor time management),
  - poor relationships (increased tension between colleagues, poor relationships with clients), and
  - increased disciplinary problems (Harnois & Gabriel, 2000; Sainsbury et al., 2008).

Findings such as these are not surprising when we consider the impact of mental illness on mood and behaviour, the stigma surrounding mental illness, and the general inability of employers/organizations to adapt to the unique needs of individual workers. Imagine waking up profoundly depressed day after day, for example. You might go to work and try to hide your thoughts and feelings due to the stigma associated with mental illness. You would likely not be able to hide your feelings consistently, and this might negatively affect your relationships with clients, colleagues, and your supervisor. Your depressed mood may alter how you think, the decisions you make, and your overall performance. You would show up as long as you could (presenteeism) even though your work life was deteriorating, which, in turn, was probably exacerbating your symptoms of depression. Eventually, you would call in sick (absenteeism), leaving your colleagues and supervisors to potentially view you in a negative light: as an unmotivated and unreliable worker, or even as a person working the system for personal gain or taking advantage of their employer and coworkers.

"It becomes a vicious cycle"

Kelly is a good example of the relationship here, as the longer a person is without work, the harder it is to even go out and look or apply for jobs. It becomes a vicious cycle of needing to work for the sake of your mental health and being unable to find work because of your mental health issues (e.g., low self-esteem). The longer one is without work, the less likely they are able to see that they are a contributing member to society.

A Practitioner in North Battleford, Saskatchewan, Canada

In addition to creating difficulties at work, mental illness can interfere with one's capacity to obtain and maintain work. Performance deficits caused by mental illness impact hiring and re-hiring, especially if the reason for those deficits is not disclosed to employers or prospective employers. If employers are aware of a candidate's mental illness concerns, then stigma that results in employers avoiding the candidate can be partially responsible for employment difficulties. Many employers, as well as job seekers, have not been educated about mental illness and equity in the workplace. Another contributor to the problem of getting work is the set of direct and indirect effects of mental illness on an individual's motivation, self-efficacy, and identity. Work-search activities such as cold calls and job interviews are difficult enough when one is healthy, energetic, confident, and secure in one's identity. This difficulty is magnified considerably when one is potentially tired, unsure, and insecure about one's identity. Thus, we can say with confidence that mental illness can interfere with work entry, participation, development or growth, and tenure.

The Impact of Work on Mental Illness

In considering the impact of work on mental illness, we must bear in mind all the complexities of mental illness described above, as well as the complexities of work and workplaces. Some work is preferable to other work, some work is more favourable for some individuals than others, some work is generally damaging, and some work is more damaging for some individuals than others.

With these considerations in mind, the evidence tells us that no *particular* mental illnesses are improved or worsened by working, but work does appear to improve overall wellbeing (Waddell & Burton, 2006). We emphasize "particular" because studies on mental illness and work tend to lump the many mental illnesses into a single category, "mental illness." Work may improve some mental illnesses and worsen others, but when put all together these effects would cancel each other out and show no overall relationship. However, Waddell and Burton's review of the literature did find that re-employment for unemployed adults is associated with fewer mental illness diagnoses, an indication that work may be helpful for some mental illnesses or may simply help ameliorate the symptoms sufficiently that illnesses go unreported and undiagnosed. Further, Brand's (2015) review of job-loss research found that job loss is associated with "higher levels of depressive symptoms, somatization, anxiety, and the loss of psychosocial assets" (p. 365). In other words, work mostly has positive effects and is good for wellbeing, but we do not have clear evidence that having or getting work reduces the onset or severity of particular mental illnesses. We do know that the loss of work is related to both mental health problems and mental illness issues (Brand, 2015; Waddell & Burton, 2006).

"He finally felt confident enough"

A participant who was referred to our program by Mental Health services was extremely anxious about applying for employment even though he was more than qualified for the positions he was applying for. It took many meetings over the course of many months, but he finally felt confident enough to apply for the job he had been aspiring for and was hired. Afterwards, his need for support from myself and his mental health counsellor was noticeably lessened immediately, and on follow-up with the participant, he shared that he felt like a weight had been lifted now that he was in the workforce.

A Practitioner in Estevan, Saskatchewan, Canada

According to Harvey et al. (2017), five issues in workplaces are clearly associated with both mental illness and mental health concerns:

- High job strain (high work demands that are on the edge of using all of one's resources)
- Lack of appropriate reward for effort (being underpaid and/or under-recognized)
- Lack of organizational justice (unfair practices in hiring, promotions, and compensation)
- Job insecurity/downsizing (situations in which workers do not know if their positions are secure and/or have seen their colleagues let go in staff-reduction efforts)
- Interpersonal problems/being bullied (being treated poorly by colleagues and/or management)

You likely have encountered many clients, as well as friends or family members, who have experienced a decline in mental health due to some or all of the above workplace problems. None of the problems necessarily trigger mental illness or cause a significant reduction in mental health, especially if they are rare and/or short-term. These problems need to persist for some time and be of a certain severity to significantly impact mental health or mental illness. Unfortunately, research has not yet uncovered *for how long and at what level of severity*.

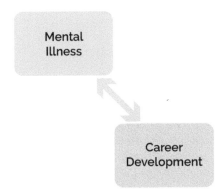

The Impact of Mental Illness on Career Development

We turn now to the relationship between mental illness and career development. First, consider "career development" as those processes you help your clients with on a daily basis, such as self-awareness, self-reflection, self-assessment, goal setting, visualization, labour market research, educational research, skill development, decision making, and the like. Career development has many components, and much of our work with clients is not obviously career development work. Frontline career development is human services work at its finest and, because of the broad range of humans served, our collective practice is creative, dynamic, and messy. Furthermore, career development happens at the individual level irrespective of contact with trained practitioners, and it does not always look like career development. Keep this in mind as you review the following evidence regarding mental illness's impact on several career development factors (in italics). Many researchers have studied mental illness and career development relationships; we have relied primarily on Boychuk, Lysaght, and Stuart (2018), Caporoso and Kiselica (2004), and Luciano and Carpenter-Song (2014) for the information provided in this section.

Self-perceptions or misappraisals of barriers to employment can be very demotivating for individuals with a mental illness. These perceptions can cause them to behave cautiously, and to avoid actions or behaviours that might be considered hostile, defensive, or otherwise off-putting by others. The end result can be a failure to engage in the career development activities leading to work and, when engaged, a negative reaction from prospective employers.

"Students need specific strategies"

Countless students over many years have presented in my Workplace Classes battling mental health issues. I have spent a good proportion of class time working with them, providing strategies to bolster self-esteem, developing confidence and promoting a growth mindset that must work effectively against the negative self-image they present with. Students need specific strategies to support the development of a positive mindset, one that will empower them emotionally and enable them to recognize and value their personal skills and attributes. On a personal level, I have witnessed many students flourish and transition successfully to the world of work when appropriate mental health and wellbeing strategies have been woven into the Career Development space.

A Practitioner in Melbourne, Victoria, Australia

Actual barriers to employment for individuals with mental illnesses are dominated by stereotypes, biases, and misunderstandings among employers, HR professionals, and recruiters, who may be reluctant to hire someone they perceive as unstable, unreliable, "too sensitive," or unable to be a team player. It is just as damaging for those same misconceptions to be held by anyone who would otherwise introduce the person with a mental illness to individuals in their networks, open learning/working doors for them, actively support them when the going gets tough, and speak highly of them to others. Consider the oft-quoted statistic about the so-called "hidden job market": 80% of jobs are not advertised. If this figure is even approximately accurate, it means that 80% of work is secured through dumb luck (i.e., walking in the door of an organization at exactly the moment someone is desperately needed and being put to work after a perfunctory interview) or through a personal connection. Eight of the ten jobs available are known to somebody, and that "somebody" needs to be willing to inform an individual of the position's availability, introduce them to the person with the authority to hire, recommend them to that person, and so on. Individuals with a mental illness, particularly a chronic and severe illness, typically have fewer "somebodies" on their side.

"We have regular meetings to make sure things are going well"

Through helping Jim attend psychiatrist and counselling appointments, along with staying committed to maintaining good mental health with self-care strategies, I was able to get him into a good place of employment. Following getting into a positive work environment it was as important to help this person maintain their mental health and continue to take care of himself. We have regular meetings to make sure things are going well. There have been incidents at work that become stressful for Jim, and there have been times that Jim has taken a stress leave from work. In the past Jim was prone to quitting the job as stress became too much instead of advocating for himself. These are some of the areas that Jim has benefited from in the help provided to him.

A Practitioner in Saskatoon, Saskatchewan, Canada

Reduced motivation to pursue work or engage in career development activities can pose serious problems for some individuals with mental illness. Motivation issues are not surprising given the daunting barriers described above. They are compounded, however, when individuals with mental illness change their *anticipated career-related outcomes*. After being diagnosed, these individuals generally see their prospects as poorer than before they were diagnosed. This may be a useful coping strategy because it lowers the demands on the person and therefore reduces stress, but it may have negative long-term consequences. *Self-confidence* among individuals with mental illness is also lower than those without mental illness, and the lack of confidence further erodes motivation.

The concerns described thus far can have a very visible impact on work-search behaviour, an important part of career development. Less visible, however, is the impact that mental illness can have on more far-reaching aspects and stages of career development. Adolescence is a pivotal period for a number of significant career development processes and outcomes. Adolescence is also when signs of mental illnesses most often emerge and are diagnosed. In fact, half of all mental disorders are diagnosed in adolescence and three quarters by the mid 20s (Kessler et al., 2007). Imagine an adolescent who has just started to experience signs or symptoms of a mental illness: The adolescent's *self-confidence* would likely be low, their willingness to engage in *exploratory behaviour* (e.g., information interviews about various work roles) would be diminished, and their ability for *identity formation* (i.e., experimenting with various roles and beginning to see one's identity crystallize) would be weak. To make things worse for the adolescent with a mental illness, they, like many of their peers, often face significant pressure to choose a career path, yet their ability to effectively make use of counselling or guidance services lessens after the onset of the illness. Given how difficult the process of exploration can be for any adolescent or young adult, the need for extra support for individuals experiencing mental illness is tremendous and underestimated.

The Impact of Career Development on Mental Illness

We noted in Chapter 3 that Keyes's dual continua model is helpful to the career development field because career development intervention may not directly affect mental illness but can bolster mental health. The evidence to date points in this direction: There is little *direct* evidence supporting a positive relationship between career development interventions and the reduction of mental illness symptoms. Most evidence focuses on mental health indicators rather than mental illness symptoms. For example, self-efficacy is related to wellbeing, and it is also known to be related to career development interventions (Robertson, 2013). There are other similar constructs linked more to mental health than mental illness that seem to be associated with career development processes. These include optimism, social identity, reduced career anxiety, and reduced cognitive dissonance.

"I am able to provide early intervention"

I have had many case examples of students (Year 9 & Year 10) missing a lot of school due to mental health issues and then start to struggle with the demands of school which leads to more pressure on their mental health. These students would come to see me (or be asked to see me by their Level Co-ordinator) and I would spend some time counselling them in regards to what the future education pathway or work pathways might look like. By talking to them and listening to them, I am able to provide early intervention of specific career development support to build their skills, confidence and resilience to face the future.

A Practitioner in Melbourne, Victoria, Australia

We cannot claim that career development interventions directly affect mental illness symptoms. In Chapter 6, "Career Development Intervention and Stress," we explore ways in which career development interventions may create mental health protective factors that mitigate against episodes of mental illness and/or alleviate the symptoms of mental illness.

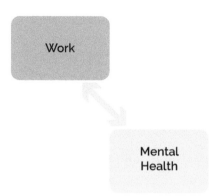

A preamble about mental health is in order before we address the relationships between mental health and work and then between mental health and career development. The operating assumption of many theorists and researchers seems to have been that mental health is on the same continuum as mental illness, contrary to Keyes's dual continua model (see Chapter 3). There has been research comparing individuals with mental illnesses to those without mental illnesses in various areas related to work and career development, but very little research on mental health as a unique variable in relationship to work and career development. Individuals without a mental illness have been considered mentally healthy, but really only by default. Mental health has been taken for granted as a norm; it is the presumed baseline on which other comparisons are made. As you will see below, this assumption has resulted in less research being conducted than one might expect.

The other interesting aspect of mental health as a variable of study is that "mental health problems" are typically poorly defined and can have a range of meanings, including "significant mental illness," "minor mental illness," "some symptoms of mental illness," and "issues preventing optimal functioning/feeling." In the discussion that follows, we attempt to specify what different researchers meant by "mental health problems," but the meaning is often unidentified or unclear.

The Impact of Mental Health on Work

There are some faint connections between mental health and work for which further research is needed. Mental health may improve or increase the ease of getting work, the ease of getting quality or suitable/fitting work, productivity at work, and longevity at work, but the literature is neither clear nor comprehensive. Bear in mind, too, that studies in this regard typically use "mental illness" as the comparator. Research focusing on the dual continua model's conception of mental health is scarce.

The Impact of Work on Mental Health

There is so much research on work's impact on physical and mental health that Gordon Waddell and Kim Burton (2006) required 257 pages to summarize it for the United Kingdom's Department of Work and Pensions in 2006. They found predominantly positive mental health outcomes resulting from work, concluding that "work and paid employment are generally beneficial for physical and mental health and well-being" (p. 10). Conversely, they also found strong evidence that unemployment is associated with poorer wellbeing, greater psychological distress, increased minor mental illness, and increased suicide attempts.

Waddell and Burton (2006) also found that re-employment of unemployed adults improves a variety of indicators of mental health, such as self-esteem and self-satisfaction. More recently, Brand's (2015) summary of research in this area confirmed Waddell and Burton's conclusions and clarified that the mental health improvements ensuing from re-employment do not bring workers back to their pre-unemployment levels of mental health right away. It can take years for workers to regain the level of mental health they had before becoming unemployed.

Of particular interest to career development practitioners is the relationship between work "fit" or "match" and mental health outcomes. Most career development theorizing is based on the concept that some work is more suitable for individuals (i.e., aligned with values, interests, skills, personality, or other attributes emphasized by the theory) than other work. The research in this regard is minimal, but it appears that job satisfaction, a key outcome of "good" or "fitting" work, is strongly and positively correlated with mental and physical health (Faragher, Cass, & Cooper, 2005). The congruence of work and interests (an attribute set that is the pivot point for John Holland's popular RIASEC model) is known to be associated, albeit only moderately, with job satisfaction (Holland, 1997). Theorists since Holland have pointed to elements other than interests, such as values, abilities, or the individual's other life roles, as important components of "fit."

In a recent paper on the meta-reviews of work and mental health (Redekopp & Huston, 2018), we summarized the research on work's contribution to mental health this way:

- Working is better than not working.
- Working in a role that fits one's strengths and proclivities is better than just working.
- Working in a fitting role within a good or decent work environment is better than just working in a fitting role.
- Working in a good and fitting role and having the capacity to adapt to and create change is better than just working in a good and fitting role. In other words, developing career development capacity is a significant wellbeing intervention. (p. 9)

The last point brings us to the relationships we are most interested in—those between career development and mental health.

The scarcity of research on the connections between career development and mental health may likely be due to theorists and researchers taking two ideas for granted:

- *Career development contributes to mental health.* An underlying and sometimes unspoken assumption of career development theories is that "good" career development (where the definition of good may vary from theory to theory) promotes mental health. If this is one's starting assumption, there is no need to study it. Frank Parsons, for example, was explicit about this assumption when he stated that aligning "best abilities and enthusiasms" with work will lay the "foundations of success and happiness" (1909, p. 3).

- *The "common" person (on whom career development theories and studies are based) is a mentally healthy person.* We have yet to find a study that asks "How does mental health influence career development?", and we suspect it is because researchers presuppose that individuals in their studies and theories are mentally healthy.

The Impact of Mental Health on Career Development

Mental health is the default starting point for theories of career development, and studies of career development interventions and processes, unless otherwise noted, assume that their subjects are mentally healthy. In the world of employment counselling, there tends to be greater recognition that mental health concerns (e.g., low self-esteem, low self-efficacy) need to be addressed in order for clients to make progress. However, even in this area, the aim is to reduce deficits rather than to examine how lesser and greater levels of flourishing impact career development activities and outcomes.

"My employer is incredible"

I have definite evidence of the above statement [that career development impacts mental health]. My employer is incredible with encouraging their employees to take mental health days, holidays, personal days and as I have "forced" myself to build this into my daily life, I have not only seen my personal mental health improve but my productivity with employment as well.

Samantha Stainer, WCG Services, Edmonton, Alberta, Canada

One of the few tested career development approaches that incorporates a mental health variable is the Action-Oriented, Hope-Centred Model of Career Development (HCMCD) developed by Spencer Niles, Norman Amundson, and Hyung Joon (Niles, Amundson, & Neault, 2011). This model takes as a given that low hopefulness, a possible indicator of poor mental health, is detrimental to career development. Hope is at the centre of HCMCD, with key career development processes (self-reflection, self-clarity, visioning, goal setting and planning, implementing and adapting) revolving around it. Thus far, tests of the model's effectiveness in improving career development outcomes—in most cases, employment—are supportive (e.g., Amundson, Goddard, Niles, Yoon, & Schmidt, 2016).

The Impact of Career Development on Mental Health

As with the understanding of mental health's impact on career development, knowledge of the impact of career development on mental health is based on assumptions and theoretical/logical connections. For example, it seems reasonable that a career development process such as self-reflection would contribute to mental health. However, there is no direct evidence that this is always the case. How do we know that self-reflection does not have an equal chance of leading to rumination, self-doubt, and despair (see, for example, Lengelle, Luken, & Meijers, 2016)?

> ## "They can see the value"
>
> A lot of the time students feel disengaged because they can't see any point in staying at school. Once they meet with a careers practitioner and they can see the value of continuing their education in order to link up with their desired pathway, their mental health improves.
>
> *A Practitioner in Melbourne, Victoria, Australia*

The lack of evidence showing the impact of career development on mental health (or our inability to find this evidence) was the impetus for our own review of the research on career development, work, mental health, and mental illness (Redekopp & Huston, 2018). In the following chapter, we propose a model based on what the field does know about the relationships between career development and mental health.

Summary

There is considerable evidence that work contributes to positive mental health, and that it does so progressively more effectively when the work "fits" with the worker, occurs in a decent work environment, and allows the worker agency and control. There is also a great deal of evidence that mental illness is a barrier to obtaining, keeping, and progressing in work, and that work has no known impact on any particular mental illness.

Far less evidence is available regarding the contribution of mental health to obtaining and keeping work, even though it is likely that mental health is a very positive contributor. Direct evidence that career development, whether formal (e.g., a career counselling session) or informal (e.g., accidental self-discovery at a worksite), is even more scarce. This paucity of research evidence is one of the key reasons we have written this book.

Reflection Questions

1. Think about times when your career was not progressing the way you wanted it to. What toll, if any, did that take on your mental health? Looking back, what would have helped you the most to minimize that toll?

2. Think about your work with clients. Roughly what percentage of your interaction with them is spent discussing or addressing the relationships among career development, work, and mental health?

3. What would you like (or need) to learn to better incorporate the myriad of relationships described in this chapter within your practice?

In theory, there is no difference between theory and practice.
In practice there is.

Yogi Berra

To Ponder...

What are the key outcomes of your work with clients?
Pick one set of these outcomes and ponder the mental
health impact of helping clients achieve them.

5. A Framework for Connecting Career Development and Mental Health

Reflect on clients you have worked with in the past year. We suspect you can picture in your mind's eye clients who worked hard to figure out what their values, interests, and beliefs were; identified their strengths and characteristics; researched sectors of the economy and possible career paths; worked on their self-management skills; developed their work-search documents; and applied for work with targeted employers. Now ask yourself this: Just before these clients went to their first interview, how did their overall mental health compare to what it was when you first started working with them? Recall Keyes's idea of mental health as distinct from mental illness when you think about this.

We anticipate that you have repeatedly witnessed clients, over time, becoming more purposeful, competent, confident, "in charge" of their own lives, sure of their ability to cope, and accepting of themselves. They probably became happier, too. Everything in this list of attributes

The core of this chapter is derived from "Connecting career development and mental health: Keynote summary," by D. E. Redekopp, 2018, *CEAV E-Journal*, *45*(3), pp. 17–20.

is a component of mental health, and gains can be made on all of these attributes regardless of whether your clients find work.

As we reviewed in Chapter 4, the evidence that work can contribute to positive mental health is overwhelming (Redekopp & Huston, 2018), with a recognition that some work can be extremely damaging to mental health. Every time we can say that we have helped a client move from unemployment to decent employment, from bad employment to better employment, or from underemployment to better employment, we can say that we have likely helped the client bolster their mental health. However, we need to be very clear with ourselves and others that we help clients with positive mental health outcomes independent of their employment status. The career development processes and activities we have our clients undertake, such as self-reflection, skill development, and planning, *whether or not these activities lead to work*, can lead to positive mental health outcomes.

This is the point at which career development theory and research become less clear about how exactly career development interventions relate to mental health outcomes, and we now propose a model that may help us all talk about these issues more effectively. The model that follows was first presented in Canada in 2017 and has been modified since. It remains open to further development and will likely look different in the future. This is the goal of theories and models—to capture current knowledge and spark further exploration and knowledge gathering. If our model does this, it will have served its purpose.

More on the Definition of Mental Health

Chapter 3, "Let's Be Clear," might have been better titled "Let's Be As Clear As We Can Be in an Area That Is Not Clear." Each term we described in Chapter 3 is messier, fuzzier, and murkier than we let on. We provided some definitions of mental health, for example, that seem quite serviceable at first glance. However, there are, in fact, many more and varied conceptions and definitions, not all of which are in alignment. One theorist might emphasize happiness as a key component of mental health whereas another may see unhappiness as an indicator of strong mental health (in instances in which individuals find themselves in unhappy circumstances).

In this chapter, we use and refer to various definitions of mental health in order to describe the ways that career development contributes to mental health. What you might see as sloppy thinking on our part—using definitions convenient for the points we are trying to make—reflects a lack of consensus and clarity in the humanities and social sciences regarding the nature of mental health. Here, then, we use definitions of mental health that assist us in making the case that career development has an impact on mental health in a variety of ways. By the end of the book, you will find that we do, eventually and tentatively, plant our career development flag on a particular mental health landscape.

A Career Development Effects Model

The model we propose sees career development processes creating five sets of outcomes or effects, each of which can be linked to positive mental health outcomes. Bear in mind that there exist many career development processes that would not be called "career development interventions." Recognize also that many career development processes can occur without a person's conscious knowledge or realization. For example, consider a student who does poorly on an assignment but is offered a chance to redo it by the teacher. The student, using the feedback from the teacher, improves the assignment and gets a better grade. On subsequent assignments for this course and for all other courses, the student carries forward the idea that assignments can be improved, that it is not impossible to do so, and that extra effort results in improved work. The student begins a pattern of working that embeds improvement prior to submitting assignments and continues this pattern through the rest of school life. This is a significant change that will alter the student's trajectory through life, but it likely would not be thought of or labelled a career development intervention.

The above distinction will help us differentiate specific interventions we might deploy with clients from those they will experience by virtue of their roles and positions in life (e.g., student, employee, citizen). Career development can be influenced by a host of actors/circumstances in many ways throughout a range of environments. For example, the ways a workplace supervisor conducts annual performance evaluations, assigns individuals to projects, provides day-to-day feedback, and shapes team interactions can each have a tremendous career development impact. These impacts are worth exploring, and many have been in fields such as human resources, organization development, occupational health and safety, and sociology. We career development practitioners may not be intervening, but it is still well worthwhile to investigate these "naturally occurring" career development processes.

The five sets of effects are as follows, in a sequence that reflects how they build on one another:

- *Life effects:* the effects of career development on an individual's life
- *Ability effects:* the skills, knowledge, and attitudes (competencies) acquired through career development processes as well as life effects
- *Self-perception effects:* the ways individuals see themselves differently due to career development processes as well as life effects and/or ability effects
- *Opportunity-perception effects:* the ways individuals see the world and the opportunities in it differently due to career development processes, life effects, ability effects, and/or self-perception effects
- *Opportunity effects:* the ways opportunities become available to individuals due to career development processes, life effects, ability effects, self-perception effects, and/or opportunity-perception effects

Figure 5.1. **Career development effects model.**

Figure 5.1 summarizes the interactions among career development processes and their effects. Career development processes, formal and informal, have an influence on all of the effects, as shown by the arrows emerging from the circle at the centre of the figure. At the same time, each set of effects contributes to new outcomes or effects, as shown by the arrows pointing from one set to the next all the way around the circle. For example, Kids in the Hall, a career development program we discuss further below, directly helped youth in Alberta, Canada, develop a variety of competencies. These competencies fall into the category of ability effects. Possessing these competencies resulted in the youth seeing themselves differently. Specifically, they displayed more confidence, greater self-efficacy, and higher self-esteem, to name some examples. Some of these changes in their self-perceptions were due to the program's ongoing career development interventions, but some of the changes would have occurred without any further intervention, simply because the youth had greater ability and recognized that their ability had improved.[6]

We make the case below that the five sets of effects in our model have something to do with mental health. In some cases, we will describe studies that show that a particular effect of career development, such as obtaining work, leads to one or more mental health outcomes. In other instances, we will show how the effect is *part of one or more definitions* of mental health. When we do so, it means that no further evidence is needed—the effect is part of the construct of mental health. We can say that, in certain realms, *career development intervention directly promotes mental health because it produces specific outcomes, such as purpose or hope, that are, by at least one popular and widely accepted definition, a feature of mental health.* Of course, beyond the definitions there is the question of face validity with all of this. Life experience, career development, and mental health are intertwined, and it is at minimum challenging, and perhaps impossible, to separate them.

To summarize, career development processes produce outcomes or effects, some of which:

- are part of an accepted definition of mental health,
- contribute to positive mental health, and/or
- contribute to other effects that in turn contribute to mental health.

Life Effects

Life effects are the outcomes associated with career development interventions/processes that directly change a person's immediate context or life circumstances. These are the effects for which the average person typically seeks the help of a career development practitioner, and there is strong evidence that these effects contribute to positive mental health. Life effects include work and some of its side effects:

---

[6] Unfortunately, the findings reported in this paragraph are observational, based on staff reports. One independent study of the program (Schnirer, Dalton, Dennis, Hartnagel, Galambos, & Bisanz, 2007), which focused predominantly on criminality, found mixed results on job-related self-efficacy (which went up in the workshops and declined when youth started actually working!) and improvement in perceived social value.

- Work
  - Moving from unemployment to employment
  - Moving from employment to better employment
- Income
- Social status/identity
- Social contact
- Time structure (pattern and predictability)
- Collective purpose
- Regular activity

We provide only a brief summary of life effects because we reviewed the effects of work on mental health in Chapter 4. We did not, however, describe the evidence tying the remaining effects to mental health. Do ponder, however, clients you have had whose overall wellbeing improved due to a steady income, a sense of place in the world, connections to others, a pattern shaping their days, and a shared purpose in the workplace.

It makes intuitive sense that some of the side effects of work contribute to mental health. Marie Jahoda (1959, 1981) proposed a model of mental health that included as components five of the side effects listed above—status/identity, social contact, structure, collective purpose, and activity (income, in her model, is not a need but a means by which needs can be met)—and noted the availability of each in work or employment settings. In Jahoda's model (Jahoda, 1959), mental health is bolstered when a person is employed because key psychological needs, that is, the five components of mental health, are met.

Jahoda's model is not universally recognized as the go-to definition or explanation of mental health. She was, however, as early as 1958, one of the first thinkers to formally raise the idea that mental health was more than the absence of mental illness. Her work has been studied extensively, particularly with regards to employment. Perhaps most recently and significantly, Zechmann and Paul (2019) completed a large, longitudinal study (more than 1,000 individuals over two years) in Germany that tested, among other concepts, the role of Jahoda's components of mental health. Their conclusion was as follows: "Employment satiates, whereas unemployment frustrates, six different psychological need variables, which pertain to mental health" (p. 15).

In other words, status/identity, social contact, structure, collective purpose, and activity are fundamental human needs that employment fulfils and that are difficult to fulfil when unemployed. Further, distress is reduced when these needs are fulfilled, thereby enhancing mental health.

We will complete our review of Zechmann and Paul's (2019) findings by foreshadowing the next two sets of effects: ability effects and self-perception effects. Zechmann and Paul's study included two additional components of mental health proposed within Deci and Ryan's self-determination theory (Deci & Ryan, 2000; Ryan, 1995): competence and autonomy. (Deci and Ryan proposed a third component, relatedness, that overlaps with Jahoda's social contact.) Deci and Ryan conceived competence as control and efficacy, and autonomy as a sense of free will and agency. Zechmann and Paul found that both competence and autonomy were strengthened when individuals were employed. These findings illustrate that work, a career development life effect, can lead directly to ability effects (in this case, Deci and Ryan's competence) and self-perception effects (i.e., autonomy as defined by Deci and Ryan). We explore these and the remaining effects below.

To summarize, work and its side effects or spin-offs can be stabilizing, identity-creating, and capacity-building forces in a person's life, fulfilling basic survival needs as well as needs of structure, belonging, and cohesion, all of which bolster mental health. However, there is much more that career development intervention contributes to positive mental health.

Ability Effects

Increasingly, the career development field is moving from a "help with decision-making" approach to a "help with the skills of managing one's own career" approach. Clients may still come to you with the expectation that you will "tell me what I should be" or "find a job for me," but you are almost certainly not going to fulfil either expectation. Rather, you will quickly work to have the client adjust their expectations as you educate them regarding career development and work-search processes. You will let the student facing a career decision know that this is a decision they need to make for themselves, and one they will make repeatedly as they and the world around them change. You will inform the work-search client that looking for work is a process involving a number of decisions and steps, a process the client needs to own and manage for themselves. They will also learn from you that it is a process they will undertake at least a few times in their working lives. In these cases, you will then help your client acquire the skills, knowledge, and attitudes they need to manage their own career development.

Most career development practice can now claim that clients will have learned career development competencies that they can take with them into the future. Practitioners can also justifiably argue that these competencies are valuable outcomes of career development practice, regardless of the client's immediate ability to obtain work. Let us consider what some of these abilities are and how they contribute to mental health outcomes.

Abilities Emerging From Career Development Interventions: A Case Study

In the mid-1990s, Dave and his company, the Life-Role Development Group Ltd., helped start a restaurant designed to help at-risk youth (e.g., street youth, young offenders) stabilize their lives and create meaningful career paths for themselves. The restaurant was operated in Edmonton, Alberta, Canada, by the Edmonton City Centre Church Corporation (now called e4c), initially as a collaboration with the Legal Aid Staff Lawyer Project (an initiative combining legal support for young people accused of crimes with help to keep their lives progressing in a positive direction). The full-service eatery was called Kids in the Hall Bistro, a play on the name of a Canadian comedy television show and the restaurant's location in Edmonton's city hall. It was open weekdays from 8 a.m. to 5 p.m. Youth in the program worked half-day shifts in the restaurant and spent the other half of the day participating in programming options such as academic upgrading, self-management workshops, career development workshops, and one-to-one counselling.

Kids in the Hall: A Summary

Kids in the Hall was an employment/education initiative for disadvantaged inner-city youth, ages 15 to 24. Participants were referred by the justice system or other agencies and typically had not completed high school (Grade 12).

The details of the program changed over its many years of operation, but the core elements remained the same:

- Half-time work in a 60-seat full-service restaurant, supervised by three, and sometimes four, paid restaurant staff
- Half-time learning/development (e.g., academic upgrading, career development and self-management), led by two career development practitioners and one youth outreach worker
- Maximum duration in the program was initially 26 weeks but later, youth could stay as long as needed

Initially funded by the governments of Canada and Alberta, as well as the Muttart Foundation, the program became about 65-70% self-sufficient through revenues and an annual fundraising gala.

Kids in the Hall operated in its core form for over 20 years and is still running today in a variant form, now called The Hallway Café & Takeaway.

Due to highly talented and dedicated restaurant and programming staff, Kids in the Hall took in hundreds of troubled youth and helped them turn their own lives around. Imagine running a restaurant with 15- to 24-year-old youth, many of whom had never eaten in a sit-down restaurant, were suspicious of adults, had few formal communication skills, had never worked, and, in some cases, had difficulty maintaining personal hygiene due to a combination of circumstances (e.g., no fixed address), habit, and skill. Through their work at the restaurant and the education/counselling they received, the youth learned how to manage their anger, communicate with customers, show up on time, develop real relationships, and work as a team, and they developed many other abilities our field would refer to as "life skills," "self-management skills," "employability skills," or "workability skills." Of course, they also learned technical skills, many of which were transferable to other work settings related to food and beverage preparation, cooking, serving, workplace safety, and customer service. Finally, they acquired career development abilities, that is, the competencies needed to manage their own career development. They learned how to create and revise a vision of a preferred future for themselves, research and plan educational pathways, explore and pursue work opportunities, and more. The gains they made were tremendous. It is difficult to convey the "shock and awe" feeling Dave had when he overheard some of the youth, for example—youth who only a few months earlier had had no address, no bank account, no job, and little hope for the future—chatting at a break about how much money they could tuck away monthly into the Retirement Savings Plans they had started!

If you run programming similar to Kids in the Hall, you know that teasing apart the effects of one part of a program (e.g., stress management training) from another (e.g., time management or conflict management training) is difficult, and it is even more difficult to differentiate the impact of formal interventions (e.g., career counselling) from those of informal interventions (e.g., truly caring and relational facilitators who "get" youth). Fortunately, for the purposes of this book, we do not need to say which intervention produced more or less change than another. We describe Kids in the Hall because it produced evidence that youth's behaviour and associated demeanour changed over time. Simple metrics from the restaurant demonstrated this: As each cohort of youth progressed through the program, attendance increased, lateness was reduced, service complaints from customers dropped, food waste was lessened, and the income/expenditure ratio increased. After a while, regular customers knew that the longer a cohort of youth had been in the program, the more they could be sure that they would be served the right order in a timely manner. An external evaluation (Schnirer et al., 2007) also provided evidence that skills and attitudes were changed by the program, leading to long-term behaviour change. For example, criminal behaviour reduced with time spent in the program, a change sustained for a year after the program ended (the maximum time of the measurement). Finally, the funders' evaluation systems determined the program to be effective, as evidenced by it becoming one of the longest-running employment preparation programs in Alberta.

Kids in the Hall did what all career development practitioners aim to do: It helped clients develop the abilities they needed to better manage their work, learning, and life pathways so that they could move toward the lives they wanted to live. What Kids in the Hall had that most practitioners do not is the luxury of long-term wrap-around programming. The intention of developing capacity, however, is the same whether working one-to-one with unemployed clients or educating students in a career-related course in high school.

We turn now to examining the three sets of abilities on which career development work focuses:

- skills needed to be employable or to reliably and successfully engage in work;
- technical skills required to meet job or work-specific requirements; and
- competencies needed to create and manage one's path through learning, work, and life.

Employability Skills

What we will call "employability skills" comprises a wide array of skills, knowledge, and attitudes related to the fundamentals of living and working in a social world. To our knowledge, there is no universally agreed-upon set of employability skills. Different organizations in different jurisdictions tend to take a pragmatic approach to creating such lists, attending to the preferences of employers in the jurisdiction and recognizing the social/cultural context of the jurisdiction. The Conference Board of Canada (https://www.conferenceboard.ca/edu/employability-skills.aspx) has a comprehensive approach that groups employability skills into three broad categories[7] as follows:

- Fundamental Skills
  - Communicate
  - Manage information

---

[7] The Department of Education in Victoria, Australia, is an example of a jurisdiction using two groupings, "employability skills" and "personal attributes" (https://www.education.vic.gov.au/Documents/school/teachers/teachingresources/careers/employabilityskills1.pdf).

- Use numbers
- Think and solve problems
- Personal Management Skills
  - Demonstrate positive attitudes and behaviours
  - Be responsible
  - Be adaptable
  - Learn continuously
  - Work safely
- Teamwork Skills
  - Work with others
  - Participate in projects and tasks

Debate and research will continue regarding the details of these skills and the degree of competence required in each. The interested reader is encouraged to review the Australian Core Skills Framework (https://research.acer.edu.au/cgi/viewcontent.cgi?article=1011&context=transitions_misc) or the Government of Canada's (2019) Essential Skills initiative (https://www.canada.ca/en/employment-social-development/programs/essential-skills.html), which not only delineate the foundational skills required to live and work in a social world but specify the level of complexity required in different work settings. Australia's core skills are learning, reading, writing, oral communication, and numeracy. Canada's essential skills are reading, writing, document use, numeracy, computer use/digital skills, thinking, oral communication, working with others, and continuous learning. Skills within each of these categories are rated in complexity on a scale of 1 to 5 in both countries. Profiles of occupations within Canada's National Occupation Classification (NOC) include essential skills. (Australian core skill levels are not included in the Australian and New Zealand Standard Classification of Occupations.) A writer of novels in Canada is presumed to have "writing" skills at a level 5, whereas a frontline employment counsellor's "writing" level typically needs to be in the 2–3 range.[8]

---

[8] The Government of Alberta's ALIS website (https://alis.alberta.ca/), particularly the OCCinfo section (https://alis.alberta.ca/occinfo/), offers a user-friendly way to explore the essential skills requirements of different occupations.

In order to connect career development with ability development and then with mental health outcomes, it is not necessary to know the specific details of the employability or essential skills clients generally acquire via career development intervention. In Chapter 8, we review instances in which you may want to be specific about the abilities your clients acquire, but for now, let us bring you back to connecting the broad set of employability skills to mental health. We mentioned Deci and Ryan's self-determination theory, which includes competence, autonomy, and relatedness as components of mental health (Deci & Ryan, 2000; Ryan, 1995). With regards to competence, they argue that humans need to have a sense of control over their environment and the ability to be efficacious within that environment—to be competent in doing what one needs to do. Clearly, insofar as the acquisition of employability skills assists individuals to function in work and social settings, it seems apparent that these skills contribute to the competence component of mental health. In fact, they do so almost by definition: Employability skills are derived from employer feedback regarding the kinds of skills they need in their workplaces. Employability skills are therefore defined as being required in workplaces, and so fit nicely into Deci and Ryan's notion of competence. Deci and Ryan are not the only theorists to postulate that competence is a component of mental health. Diener and Biswas-Diener (2008), Ryff (1989), and Westerhof and Keyes (2010) each include mastery over one's environment as a component of mental health. Related to mastery is Martin Seligman's (2012) notion of accomplishment, one of his five components of his version of flourishing.

In short, career development interventions very often build client capacity regarding employability, and the ensuing employability skills contribute to the competence that aligns with several definitions of mental health. Some career development interventions that build this capacity may not be labelled "career development" services. Consider experiential learning, such as the community service learning, internships, cooperative education, or work-integrated learning increasingly being offered in secondary and post-secondary schools. These initiatives help students develop both "soft" employability skills and technical work skills.

Technical Skills

Career development programming, particularly employment programming, often includes or connects with technical training, where "technical" often means the skills needed to use the core terminology and tools/equipment (e.g., measuring tape or laser, espresso machine, debit machine) of an area of work (e.g., construction, coffee shop, retail store). These skills enable workers to enter an industry with some knowledge under their belts so that their first foray into paid work in that industry is less likely to provoke anxiety and more likely to be successful. The Kids in the Hall program, for example, taught youth a variety of technical skills—how to properly use a knife, knowledge of menu ingredients, how to take an order—that are specific to the restaurant industry.[9] We will not elaborate on the mental health outcomes related to becoming competent in technical skills. Suffice it to say that the environmental mastery or competence portion of mental health is likely to be strengthened with these skills. This has been visibly evident, for example, in every Kids in the Hall fundraising gala in which the youth put on a five-course, $150/plate dinner. The youths' pride in their ability to create, plate, and serve a dinner worthy of any restaurant in town is palpable. You have seen this pride, too, if you run programs of this nature. We have not found research, however, that connects specific technical competence to mental health. However, if being technically competent relates to environmental mastery, which is included in some definitions of mental health, then technical competence qualifies as a potential determinant of mental health.

Career Management Skills

Broad-based career development services aim to enable clients to learn the skills, knowledge, and attitudes they need to manage, as much as context will allow, their own career development. Developmental theorists such as Ginzberg, Ginsburg, Axelrad, and Herma (1951) and Donald Super (1957) initially led the shift in thinking from career development as a point-in-time vocational choice to career development as an ongoing process throughout life that started long before the

---

[9] One of the reasons a restaurant was chosen as a built-in work experience for youth was the significant transferability of technical skills to other roles and sectors. "Take a lunch order" may be a restaurant-specific ability, but "customer service skills" permeate most industries.

individual entered the world of work. Viewing career as a developmental phenomenon resulted in theorizing about the related skills, knowledge, and attitudes that develop over the lifespan, how they develop, and how they need to change over time and in different contexts.

In the United States, thinking of career development as requiring different abilities over time led the National Occupational Information Coordinating Committee (NOICC) in the 1980s to create a very practical resource, the *National Career Development Guidelines* (Lankard, 1991). The crux of the guidelines were 12 competencies within three career development areas: self-knowledge, educational and occupational exploration, and career planning. The developmental nature of each competency was reflected in a four-level framework, roughly corresponding to the ages associated with elementary school, middle school, high school, and adulthood. Canada obtained permission to modernize and adapt the guidelines in the 1990s, resulting in the *Blueprint for Life/Work Designs* (Haché, Redekopp, & Jarvis, 2006). Shortly thereafter, the *Blueprint* was adapted and revised for use in Australia and England, and it informed similar approaches in New Zealand and Scotland. Most recently, the European Union's LEADER (LEarning And DEcision Making Resources) project involved Greece, Italy, Romania, Spain, Turkey, and the United Kingdom in updating and contextualizing career management competencies (Neary, Dodd, & Hooley, 2015).

We provide this brief history to illustrate that the mapping out of career management competencies is very much a work in process. The time it takes to move from theory to practice to evidence (and not always in that order) is also highlighted by the chronology above. The theoretical work of the 1950s is still not being fully implemented or measured, and a host of new theories and approaches to career development have since been developed. As you will see below, the lag-time between theory and evidence is long, therefore much of the work on career development abilities continues to be speculative.

LEADER career management skills framework

1. Personal effectiveness
- I know who I am and what I am good at.
- I'm able to reflect on my strengths and address my weaknesses.
- I make effective decisions relating to my life, learning and work.
- I remain positive when facing setbacks and I keep a positive orientation to the future.
- I make use of appropriate technologies to develop my career.
- I generate ideas that help me to achieve my goals.
- I can match my skills to labour market needs.
- I can perform the appropriate actions and activities needed to cope effectively with career issues.

2. Managing relationships
- I find and utilise information and the support of others.
- I assess the pros and cons of formal and informal sources of information.
- I interact confidently and effectively with others.
- I build professional relationships and networks that support my career.
- I maintain my professional relationships and networks.
- I use the social media networks (social networking skills).

3. Finding work and accessing learning
- I learn throughout life.
- I can find work and successfully manage selection processes (job search skills).
- I create opportunities and alternative career perspectives to build my career.
- I create synergies in my career.
- I know how to negotiate a job or cooperation.
- I can cope and "negotiate" successfully with changes and transitions in the world of work (career adaptability).

4. Managing life and career

- I can decide on and to set my career/life goals within appropriate timescales.
- I manage my goals, my time and personal finances in a way that supports my career building.
- I adapt my varied roles, jobs responsibilities, schedules and context.
- I am innovative and creative in my thinking about my work, learning and life.
- I maintain a balance in my life, learning and work that is right for me.
- I manage to face transitions in a flexible and adaptable way.
- I can cope with adversities and changes which take place in life and career exactly at the moment they occur (career resilience).

5. Understanding the world

- I understand how changes in society, politics and the economy relate to my life, learning and work.
- I understand how life, learning and work roles change over time.
- I can act effectively as a part of the society as a whole (social awareness).
- I identify, create and capitalize on fortuitous situations, either positive or negative ones (readiness to happenstance).
- I can act at an international level for issues related to my life, learning and work (mobility skills).

Figure 5.2. **LEADER career management skills framework.** From "Understanding Career Management Skills: Findings from the First Phase of the CMS LEADER Project," by S. Neary, V. Dodd, and T. Hooley, 2015, p. 46.

A quick glance at the list of career management competencies or skills drafted by the LEADER project (see Figure 5.2) reveals a direct connection to mental health. Recall the wellbeing components that define mental health in Keyes's model: emotional, social, and psychological (Keyes, 2005; Westerhof & Keyes, 2010). Let us look at how LEADER's career management competencies contribute to each of these.

- "Personal effectiveness" competencies such as "I know who I am and what I am good at," "I'm able to reflect on my strengths and address my weaknesses," "I make effective decisions relating to my life, learning, and work," and "I remain positive when facing setbacks and I keep a positive orientation to the future" reflect elements of psychological wellbeing: self-acceptance, personal growth, environmental mastery, and autonomy.

- "Managing relationships" competencies such as "I find and utilise information and the support of others," "I interact confidently and effectively with others," "I build professional relationships and networks that support my career," and "I maintain my professional relationships and networks" are all part of developing and maintaining positive relationships, an element of Keyes's psychological wellbeing. They also contribute to all five components of Keyes's social wellbeing: acceptance (positive attitude toward others), actualization (belief in community's potential), contribution (feeling of value), coherence (ability to make meaning of society), and integration (belonging).

- "Finding work and accessing learning" competencies, particularly "I learn throughout life" and "I can cope and 'negotiate' successfully with changes and transitions in the world of work (career adaptability)" speak to the psychological wellbeing elements of personal growth, environmental mastery, and autonomy. The competencies related to finding work also facilitate the ability to gain employment, which is associated with its own set of mental health outcomes as described in Chapter 4.

- The competencies within "Managing life and career" directly address psychological wellbeing elements of growth, mastery, and autonomy, and indirectly include the element of purpose in life as well.

- "Understanding the world" competencies are tied to social wellbeing, particularly the idea of coherence or being able to make meaning of societal events.

Clearly, some career development interventions will develop career management competencies more deeply and widely than others. A program such as Kids in the Hall can effect more change in competence than a service that helps executives refine their resumés.

These differences will be revealed in due time with ongoing evidence-gathering, addressed in Chapter 10. However, we encourage you to not dismiss the potential impact on mental health of seemingly minor career development interventions, such as helping someone polish a resumé. All interventions have the potential to develop a career management competency that may then help the individual see the need to work on another competency, which then leads to another, and so on. All interventions may also create a shift in a person's thinking about who they are, what they believe about themselves, and what they believe about the world. A seemingly small shift in belief can, like a snowball rolling down a snowy hill, become something much larger and significant. Shifts in beliefs are the core of the next set of outcomes, self-perception effects.

In brief, when career development interventions develop career management competencies (and they should in most cases), they will almost always directly bolster either psychological wellbeing, social wellbeing, or both. Also, career management competencies are presumed to enable individuals to more ably live the life they want to live. If this is correct, developing career management competencies will also lead to emotional wellbeing: positive affect, happiness, and life satisfaction.

Self-Perception Effects

You are pleased but not surprised when an aimless, dispirited, and seemingly feckless client leaves your career development program, intervention, classroom, or office with a sense that they want to change, can change, and have a direction for the change they want in their lives. You know that clients see themselves differently after being involved in career development interventions, particularly if they have acquired career management competencies (and know they have done so) and more so if they have obtained work or meaningful training/education. In this section, we review some key self-perception changes targeted by career development interventions and their relationship to mental health.

Self-efficacy: I Can Do This

Albert Bandura, born in Mundare, Alberta (a town now famous for its giant statue of a sausage), is one of the most cited psychologists in the world, up there with Sigmund Freud, Jean Piaget, B.F. Skinner, and Carl Rogers. One of the many reasons his work is so often cited is because it includes theory and research on a central belief affecting almost all behaviour: self-efficacy. Often confused with self-esteem, self-efficacy is the belief system an individual has about their ability to accomplish tasks and achieve goals, and specifically the belief that "I can accomplish the tasks before me" (Bandura, 1986). Self-esteem, which we discuss below, is a belief about value or worth. One might expect that a person with a high level of self-efficacy would also have high self-esteem, but this need not be the case. You likely have had clients who have no hesitation in getting things done or persisting at difficult tasks (two indicators of self-efficacy) and yet do not feel great about themselves or their accomplishments. You have probably also worked with people who feel positive about themselves (self-esteem) yet are tentative about their ability to accomplish tasks and give up easily when the going gets rough.

Self-efficacy is important to mental health in a number of ways. Here we focus on only two:

1. *Self-efficacy is either synonymous with, or highly related to, the psychological wellbeing element of environmental mastery.* In other words, self-efficacy is a direct indicator of a component of mental health.

2. *Self-efficacy plays a pivotal role in all of an individual's endeavours* (this is discussed further in the next chapter). Quite simply, self-efficacy beliefs can act like an "on-off switch" for behaviour. People are far less likely to start a course of action if they think they cannot successfully complete it than if they think they can. Consider this in terms of choices such as selecting courses in school, attending post-secondary education, cold-calling for information interviews, going to job interviews, taking on a new job, accepting a promotion, or even going on a date.

Self-efficacy is therefore both a component of mental health as well as a prerequisite to, or corequisite of, other components of mental health.

Do we have evidence that career development intervention generally influences self-efficacy? The answer is yes. Akkermans, Brenninkmeijer, Schaufeli, and Blonk (2015), for example, found that young employees participating in CareerSKILLS, a program based on career competencies, developed greater self-efficacy than did participants in a control group. Kerr and Kurpius (2004) developed an intervention for young at-risk women emphasizing career identity and exploration; they found self-efficacy, predictions of self-efficacy in the future, and self-esteem were significantly increased. More recently, CareerAdvance, a program helping low-income parents enter the health care field, was shown to help individuals increase their self-efficacy as compared to a matched-comparison group (Chase-Lansdale et al., 2019). Also recently, Yoon, Bailey, Amundson, and Niles (2019) found that refugees' self-efficacy increased, as compared to a control group, in a career development program based on Hope-Action Theory. These examples, which include young at-risk women, young employees, low-income parents, and unemployed refugees, demonstrate that different career development interventions can generate increased self-efficacy in a variety of groups.

A concept related to self-efficacy is the theory of mindset (Dweck, 1999; see sidebar for more), which proposes a spectrum ranging from "fixed" to "growth." People with a fixed mindset attribute success to stable traits (e.g., "I am smart") while those with a growth mindset believe success results from changeable skills or effort (e.g., "If I work harder, I will do better"). A person's mindset, or set of beliefs, can have a tremendous influence on their behaviour. In your practice, you have no doubt had clients with mindsets at either end of the spectrum, and you know how difficult it can be to work with a client whose mindset is fixed, whether negatively (e.g., "I am too old to change") or positively (e.g., "I am God's gift to employers!"). As you have likely surmised, a growth mindset is conceptually aligned with self-efficacy, but the research on the relationship between mindset and self-efficacy is not entirely clear. We focus on self-efficacy in our model because of the vast amount of research supporting the construct and because it is directly used in mental health conceptualizations. However, mindset research is well worth following as it offers a different lens through which to view a similar notion, and it does so in a way that has intuitive appeal for your clientele.

More on Mindsets

According to the theory of mindset, the attributions people make about their success can have direct and longlasting effects on behaviour. For example, a person with a fixed mindset with regard to test-writing ("I'm a smart test-writer") who then fails a number of tests may change their mindset ("I'm not a smart test-writer") and avoid future situations in which tests are required. A person with a growth mindset who fails a number of tests is more likely to put energy into figuring out how to become a better test-writer.

How people explain cause and effect to themselves is overwhelmingly important in human behaviour and is a topic we will return to later in this chapter and the next. H. B. Gelatt, a career-decision-making theorist, uses the phrase "I'll see it when I believe it" to illustrate how beliefs shape not only behaviour, but even how people perceive their worlds.

The research on the relationship between mindset and self-efficacy is inconclusive. For example, in comparing two groups of students, one participating in an intervention to boost a growth mindset and one control, Rhew, Piro, Goolkasian, and Cosentino (2018) found that improvement in growth mindset was accompanied by increased motivation to learn but not self-efficacy. These results and others like them (e.g., Glerum, Loyens, & Rikers, 2018) are perplexing and point to the need for more study.

Self-Esteem and Self-Acceptance: I Feel Okay About Myself

Self-esteem, the general evaluation of one's worth, and self-acceptance, the ability to hold oneself in positive regard regardless of particular achievements and characteristics, are distinct but related concepts. Both speak to how individuals feel about themselves, but both approach the aim to "feel okay about myself" differently. To feel okay via self-esteem, individuals have to evaluate themselves as worthy, which means doing worthy things (things they perceive as worthy) or having valuable characteristics (characteristics they perceive as valuable) and then being aware of these perceptions. To feel okay via self-acceptance, individuals need to let go of their appraisals of worth and value and be okay with who they are, warts and all.

Interestingly, self-esteem is not a component of dominant definitions of mental health except insofar as it influences emotional wellbeing elements such as positive affect, happiness, and life satisfaction. Thinkers such as Jahoda, Keyes, and Ryff each have self-acceptance as an indicator of mental health, but self-esteem does not enter into their definitions.

You may be wondering why we bring up a characteristic that is not a notable part of existing definitions and models of mental health. We do so because our experience, as well as some research, tells us that career development practitioners believe that developing self-esteem is an important aim of their work, and that their work achieves this aim reasonably reliably. For example, the Canadian Career Development Foundation worked, and is still working, on developing a set of common indicators of the outcomes of career development practice (Bezanson, Goyer, Michaud, Redekopp, & Savard, 2014; Redekopp, Bezanson, & Dugas, 2013; Redekopp, Bezanson, & Dugas, 2015). These common indicators would potentially cut across interventions, clients, settings, and geography, thereby allowing practitioners, researchers, and policy-makers across the country to measure the same things and make apples-to-apples comparisons of different approaches. Currently, Canada (as well as Australia) has, at best, apples-to-oranges comparisons of most interesting outcomes other than "employment" and "in training," making meaningful evaluation quite difficult. To launch the development of common indicators, literature was reviewed to identify dominant inputs, processes, and outcomes measured in career development practice, and then focus groups were conducted with Canadian career development practitioners to narrow down a broad list of items to a smaller, more manageable set. After going through a lengthy list of possible variables indicating important client change, practitioners focused on self-management, wellbeing (in the sense of quality of life), self-efficacy, self-awareness, and self-esteem. To practitioners, self-esteem is an important indicator of change because it is quite palpable (i.e., practitioners can see/feel when their clients begin to see themselves in a more positive light) and it provides their clients with some of the energy they need to keep moving, overcome obstacles, and stay the course. At minimum, practitioners know that low self-esteem can be an enormous impediment to change and growth.

For practitioners, self-esteem is an "in your face" variable that cannot be ignored. We have therefore discussed it here but will make little reference to it as we proceed (although we come back to it in the discussion of coping in the next chapter). This is not because we think it is unimportant or should not be measured, but because it is currently not part of dominant definitions and models of mental health. Self-acceptance, however, is woven into several definitions and so that is where we will focus our attention.

A problem with focusing on self-acceptance, at least from our perspective, is that there is virtually no research connecting career development intervention with self-acceptance. Aiello and Tesi (2017) and Strauser, Lustig, and Çiftçi (2008) studied the impact of self-acceptance on work engagement and career development, respectively, but we could find only one study that assessed the impact of career development on self-acceptance: Peck (1975) studied the effects of a career education project in Washington, DC, inner-city elementary schools, finding year-over-year improvements in self-acceptance.

Identity: I Know Who I Am

Identity and related constructs have been central in career development theory.

- Donald Super (1957) saw career development as the development and maintenance of self-concept in relationship to life's various roles.

- John Holland's (1973) RIASEC model is based on the idea that personality is composed of one's interests. Matching personality to corresponding work environments is important to career success, and identity is defined by the clarity and stability of personality characteristics.

- Bright and Pryor's (2011) chaos theory of careers situates identity as unique to each individual and continuously adjusting as the individual's nature interacts with constantly changing environmental circumstances.

- Mark Savickas's (2011) career construction theory has an approach to identity and self that is quite nuanced: Savickas sees the self as larger than identity; identity is formed as the self negotiates with and adjusts to a social world. Identity is both created and described through narrative or story, and these stories serve to shape career decisions and behaviours.

Although the theorists listed above have different conceptions of identity and are certainly not in complete agreement about the various uses of the term, it is clear that identity as a construct is important in career development. The self (i.e., the entity to which self-esteem, self-acceptance, and self-efficacy refer) sees itself in certain ways, ways that likely depend on inherent characteristics (nature), experiences (nurture), and dynamic needs related to fitting into a social/cultural world. The identity that emerges may change over time, but it serves the purpose of "framing" the self in a way that is communicable, socially acceptable, and consistent. If we view identity in this general way, as the means by which the self can capture, understand, and communicate key elements of self that fit within a social environment, it then becomes easy to see that career development intervention often works directly to

- identify and differentiate elements of identity (e.g., interests, values, beliefs);

- stabilize or bolster identity by providing labels regarding personality, interests, preferences, and other characteristics (e.g., Realistic-Investigative-Artistic, ENTJ, introvert); and

- create concise derivations of one's identity for the purposes of marketing within specific contexts (i.e., with an elevator speech) and work-search documentation (e.g., "I am a goal-oriented salesperson driven by results").

Whether or not forming, clarifying, and/or crystallizing identity contributes to mental health is the next issue to address. "Identity" is not a criterion of mental health in the definitions we reviewed, so we need to look for signs of identity in related components of mental health. The place to do this, particularly given Savickas's (2011) view of identity as a construct that is negotiated between the self and social/cultural circumstances, is in Westerhof and Keyes's (2010) category of social wellbeing. Recall the five elements of social wellbeing:

1. *Social coherence:* being able to make meaning of what is happening in society

2. *Social acceptance:* a positive attitude toward others while acknowledging their difficulties

3. *Social actualization:* the belief that the community has potential and can evolve positively

4. *Social contribution:* the feeling that one's activities contribute to and are valued by society

5. *Social integration:* a sense of belonging to a community

Where items 1–3 focus on society, items 4 and 5, social contribution and social integration, refer to the relationship between the individual and society. Identity seems to be particularly relevant here because it is the means by which the self communicates to society what it has to offer and why it should belong. An unclear identity may not prevent social contribution and social integration entirely, but as career development practitioners have repeatedly seen, the ability to understand, articulate, communicate, and adjust one's identity to fit different contexts while remaining "true" to oneself is enormously helpful in finding ways to contribute and fitting into a social group. Clarity about one's identity affords a better understanding of one's fit and value in the social world and likely contributes to Keyes's social wellbeing and thereby to mental health.

Hope: I'll Be Okay No Matter What Happens

When you see the word "hope," you may be inclined to equate it with "optimism," or feeling positive about the future. Here, we use a definition of hope widely used within mainstream psychology: "a positive motivational state that is based on an interactively derived sense of successful (a) agency (goal-directed energy) and (b) pathways (planning to meet goals)" (Snyder, Irving, & Anderson, 1991, p. 287). Where optimism, which we address below, is about a better future, hope is about conceiving one's own ability to reach goals regardless of what the future holds. If optimism is "tomorrow will be a better day," hope is "I'll be fine no matter what tomorrow brings."

One way to think of hope is as a state of long-range self-efficacy ("I can do that") in which upcoming tasks are unknown. Another way to think of hope is to see it as coping-in-the-future. In typical use, "coping" refers to thoughts and strategies with regard to meeting immediate demands (e.g., going on-stage to give a talk to a large audience) or near-future demands (e.g., a test a week from now). Hope is the ability to think that coping will occur in the future, a time at which we do not really know the demands we will face.

As a practitioner, you undoubtedly have witnessed many, if not most, clients leave your care with more hope than when they started. We suspect that you consider increased hope as almost a given of your practice, a natural outcome of the work you do. Assumed outcomes tend to not be measured, and only recently has research regarding career development and hope proliferated. Leading the charge on this front have been Norm Amundson and Spencer Niles with what they now refer to as Hope-Action Theory (HAT) (Niles, Amundson, & Yoon, 2019). Hope-Action Theory conceives hope to be both a precursor and an outcome of career development. As a precursor, it provides the motivational energy to undertake career development activities (in HAT, these are self-reflection, self-clarity, visioning, goal setting and planning, and implementing and adapting). These activities, when successful, generate the outcome of greater levels of hope.

Having a theory that explicitly connects career development and hope has and will generate research connecting the two concepts. Amundson, Niles, and their collaborators' research initiatives are finding that career development intervention increases hope. For example, Yoon, Bailey, Amundson, and Niles (2019) used HAT to develop a program for refugees, finding that those in the program increased their levels of hope more than did a control group. The model was also used to develop a program for internationally educated professionals and, again, was found to increase levels of hope (Clarke, Amundson, Niles, & Yoon, 2018). The research emerging from work on HAT is still in its infancy but thus far is providing evidence that career development intervention increases hope and that HAT has merit as a theory.

Several other researchers have connected hope with career development but with mixed results. Hirschi, Abessolo, and Froidevaux (2015) studied over 200 first-year university students, anticipating that increased hope would lead to increased career exploration, and that career exploration would, in turn, generate more hope. They indeed found that hope and career exploration are positively correlated, but neither appears to cause changes in the other. Instead, their study suggested that some other variable, perhaps personality or a social variable, causes both hope and career exploration to rise or fall. More recently, however, Ginevra and Nota (2018) tested a 10-unit career development intervention with children (about 10 years old, on average) and found increased hope after the intervention. Santilli, Nota, and Hartung (2019) used a career construction intervention with early adolescents but did not find changes in hope.

More research is clearly needed to establish the relationships between career development and hope. Assuming for a moment that career development does enhance hope, we will turn to the relationship between hope and mental health. This is an interesting turn: No major psychological, sociological, or health agency definition of mental health includes hope as a component or criterion! Diener and Biswas-Diener (2008) have "future orientation," which includes hope and optimism, as one of their dimensions of mental health, but theirs is not a dominant definition of mental health. Given how immediately we and the career development practitioners we have worked with over the years connect hope to mental health, its omission from definitions of mental health perplexes us.

To find hope in the definitions, we are best served to view it as a long-term projection of coping—as an expectation to cope in the future. Coping is prevalent within health agency definitions of mental health, including the definitions from the World Health Organization, the Australian Government Department of Health and Ageing, and the Public Health Agency of Canada presented in Chapter 3. In these definitions, mental health is partially indicated by the ability to cope and handle life's demands. If the ability to cope and handle life's demands includes an expectation to do so in the future, then hope could also be an indicator of mental health.

If hope is conceived as "perceptions of coping in the future," it is imperative that our field shows the connections between career development practice and levels of hope. Strategic career development—managing today's demands and opportunities in ways that lead to more desirable opportunities over time—should create the virtuous cycle that Hirshi et al. (2015) predicted, whereby hope increases motivation to engage in career development activities such as career exploration, and these activities in turn increase hope.

Purpose: I Have a Reason/Reasons for Being

Unlike the concept of hope, "purpose" or "meaning" is found in a variety of conceptions of mental health, including those of Antonovsky (1987), Diener and Biswas-Diener (2008), Keyes (Westerhof & Keyes, 2010), Ryff (1989), and Seligman (2012). Having one or more reasons for being seems to be a core element of the positive human condition. Being purposeless is not a mental illness, but the theorists listed here would argue that it is a sign of languishing or incomplete fulfilment.

Career development practice can aim both directly and indirectly at purpose or meaning. In the broadest sense, career development practice helps individuals live the lives they want to live or certainly make progress in that direction. Presumably, this desired life includes a purpose or several purposes that can be fulfilled at work, in the community, and in the personal/family sphere. This is important: The career development practitioner's aim is not necessarily that each client find completely fulfilling and purposeful work. The aim is that the individual's "constellation of life roles," a phrase coined by Donald Super (1957), fit and move together in ways desirable to the individual. For some clients, work is a means to an end; they find their purpose elsewhere. For others, their current work is a stepping stone to more prestigious work; their purpose may lie in the upward movement. Others want their work role to be meaningful or purposeful in and of itself. Amy Wrzesniewski (Wrzesniewski, McCauley, Rozin, & Schwartz, 1997) labels these three orientations to work "job orientation," "career orientation," and "calling orientation," respectively.

The Three Bricklayers: A Story About Choice

You have likely heard the centuries-old story, attributed to Sir Christopher Wren, the great architect of St. Paul's Cathedral in London, about encountering three bricklayers on a scaffold. One crouched, working slowly; one was half-standing, working a little more quickly; and one was standing tall and working very quickly. Wren apparently asked each "What are you doing"? The crouching bricklayer said, "I'm working, I'm a bricklayer." The second said, "I'm building a wall." The most productive bricklayer answered, "I'm building a cathedral to the Almighty."

This story is often used in management and leadership training to illustrate how employees need to see the bigger context of their work and personally relate to this context. The story is told in the hope that managers will help their employees see how their work contributes to the organization's vision, which managers certainly should do. What is often missed, however, is that an employee's perspective is a choice. The "I'm a bricklayer" employee will not change their perspective by looking at the blueprint of the finished cathedral. They will change their perspective when they see how their choices can help them better live the life they want to live—a career development task.

The key for our purposes is that career development practice helps individuals find avenues by which to pursue purpose and meaning. Also, career development practice done well helps clients recognize that they *create* rather than find purpose and meaning. Individuals can choose work because they view it as purposeful, and they can create purpose in work that initially did not feel purposeful. Savickas's (2011) career construction theory may be the exemplar here. For Savickas, career is a story (what happened) with a plot (why it happened) and a theme (what it means). Individuals can choose to create meaning in anything they do, and career development practitioners can help them with these choices.

The evidence supports the claim that career development interventions enable purposefulness. Duffy, Douglass, Autin, and Allan (2014) surveyed adults three times over six months, with over 200 completing all three surveys. Duffy et al. were expecting that "living a calling" (which they defined as an "integral part of their life meaning" [p. 605]) would enhance career commitment, work meaning, and job satisfaction. Instead, they found that meaningful and satisfying work as well as career commitment enhanced "living a calling." In other words, the outcomes of effective career development—selecting and committing to a career path, choosing meaningful work, and finding a satisfying environment in which to engage in that work—create calling or purpose, not the other way around.

Career development, whether it results from a career intervention or from one's initiative, facilitates the development of a sense of purpose. We can take that connection as a fact. Does a sense of purpose, which is part of some definitions of mental health, lead to additional positive mental health outcomes? There is limited direct research, but we can connect some of the dots. In a large (n = 3,489) longitudinal study of midlife individuals, Lewis, Turiano, Payne, and Hill (2017) found a significant relationship between one's sense of purpose and cognitive function. Specifically, individuals with a greater sense of purpose also produced higher scores in memory, executive functioning, and overall cognitive function. Each of these measures is related to positive mental health, and executive function is obviously connected to processes and outcomes of career development intervention. By definition, executive function refers to a set of cognitive functions that include one's ability to plan, make decisions, selectively attend, and integrate prior learning (Chan, Shum, Toulopoulou, & Chen, 2008). In short, formal and informal career development processes generate a sense of purpose, purpose is related to executive function and other cognitive abilities, and cognitive abilities are related to mental health.

Further evidence for a relationship between sense of purpose and positive mental health comes from a large (n = 6,840) study of teachers in China that found that those with a greater sense of purpose also had better health (Li et al., 2016). The study determined that greater health measures resulted from an enhanced capacity to manage stress. Teachers with a greater sense of purpose were more stress resilient and, accordingly, reported better health. As we will discuss in the next chapter, although there is an optimal level of stress for most people, it is usually the case that less stress is associated with positive mental health.

To summarize this review of self-perception effects, we can reasonably and safely claim that career development interventions and processes can enhance the following factors, each of which is directly related to mental health:

- Self-efficacy
- Self-esteem and self-acceptance
- Identity
- Hope
- Purpose/meaning

Opportunity-Perception Effects

The work of career development practitioners results in clients seeing the world differently. Career development practitioners readily claim that their work increases individuals' abilities to see more opportunities, more meaningful and relevant opportunities, and more accessible opportunities, especially in the world of work. You have likely worked with many individuals who were feeling anxious about their futures, such as a student feeling pressure to "decide what they should be" or an unemployed adult in need of a source of income. You undoubtedly helped them move from a myopic focus on a very limited range of options (e.g., "I want to be an artist but my parents want me to be a lawyer" or "I need a job in my community that pays at least a living wage and where I can start next week") to consideration of a broad but manageable range of options. You know, for example, that reviewing all occupations (over 40,000!) would be overwhelming, but you also know that "X or Y" choices are far too limiting.

Unfortunately, the great efforts you and thousands of your colleagues undertake in this regard have gone largely unmeasured. What we in the field believe to be true—that we enable our clients to see a broader range of options, manage the uncertainty inherent in thinking about the future, and free up some of their thinking powers by lessening their anxiety and fear—have not been dominant topics of research. What we have some evidence for is that career development intervention can enhance optimism, the "belief that future events are likely to have positive outcomes" (Yue, Hiranandani, Jiang, Hou, & Chen, 2017, p. 641). In a study cited earlier, Chase-Lansdale et al. (2019) found increased levels of optimism in their group of low-income parents after a career development program compared with a control group. Similarly, Ginerva and Nota's (2018) study with children found optimism increasing with a career development intervention as compared to a control group. Spurk, Kauffeld, Barthaurer, and Heinemann (2015), in a study exploring career development intervention with female academics working in STEM fields at German universities, found that variations of networking interventions and coping produced career optimism. Santilla, Nota, and Hartung (2019), however, found no change in optimism with either adolescents undertaking a traditional group career-development intervention or a group career-construction intervention.

Optimism likely develops incidentally or indirectly in a great deal of career development practice. Career development practitioners, whether intentionally or unintentionally, help clients think differently about themselves and the world. You have almost certainly challenged clients' beliefs, for example, that "there are no jobs out there," "I don't have any transferable skills," or "nobody will hire me with my criminal convictions on record." As noted in the discussion of mindsets earlier, beliefs are enormous influences on behaviour, particularly when the beliefs are about attributions of cause and effect. Martin Seligman's (1990) early work on "learned optimism" illustrates some of this power of attribution in explaining optimists and pessimists. He found that optimists and pessimists explain success and failure to themselves within three categories:

- Personal – something within me caused the outcome
- Permanence – the result will not change over time
- Pervasiveness – this situation applies to all situations

Each category is polarized (personal versus not personal, permanent versus temporary, pervasive versus specific). Optimists and pessimists go to one pole or another to explain successes and failures, but they do so *in opposite ways*. For example, one of your clients goes to a job interview and does not get the job. If the client is prone to pessimism, the client will say to themselves (and perhaps to you) something such as "I'm really not good in interviews (personal). I've done a lot of them badly and I'll always do them badly (permanent). It doesn't matter whether I'm interviewing for a job, a volunteer position, or to get an apartment—I'll do it poorly (universal pervasiveness)." The optimist takes the opposite approach: "I did pretty well in the interview but the interviewer seemed to be really distracted (external, not personal). I think they were just having a bad day (temporary, not permanent). It was good practice for the volunteer position I'm seeking; I'm sure I'll do well in that interview (specific, not universally pervasive).

What's particularly interesting is that the polarities of their attributions *switch* when they are successful! The pessimist talks to themselves about success as externally caused (e.g., luck), temporary, and specific to a situation. For the optimist, success is because of personal causes, will be achieved again in time, and will transfer to other situations.

We have explored Seligman's ideas about optimism not because he has the final say on the matter, but rather to illustrate that you and other career development practitioners may be playing a significant role in changing clients' beliefs about themselves and the world. We suspect you do not measure these changes; they are simply an integral element of what you do. However, these beliefs may have a very long reach in terms of the success of your clients in various situations above and beyond the presenting issue that brought them to your service.

Further research is definitely needed to determine whether practitioners' experiences with the following opportunity-perception effects are substantiated:

- *Career development intervention helps individuals better tolerate uncertainty and ambiguity.* H. B. Gelatt's "positive uncertainty" will likely be a key component of this research (Gelatt & Gelatt, 2003).
- *Career development intervention helps widen individuals' "cognitive bandwidth."* Cognitive bandwidth (Mullainathan & Shafir, 2013) refers to the amount of cognitive processing power available to a person after their core concerns are addressed. In other words, career development intervention helps reduce anxiety about the future and in so doing allows people to use more of their cognitive powers—powers that were being diverted into handling anxiety. Another way to think of this is in terms of Barbara Frederickson's (2004) "broaden-and-build theory of positive emotions." Frederickson argues that negative emotions, such as fear and anxiety, narrow one's ability to see their environment. As feelings of safety, comfort, and positive anticipation increase, one's perceptual horizons widen. Individuals can see more in their environment than they could when they were anxious or afraid.

It is not entirely clear that uncertainty tolerance and increased cognitive bandwidth contribute directly to positive mental health, but a strong argument could be made that both effects increase a person's abilities to cope and therefore better manage life's demands, thus contributing indirectly to better mental health.

Opportunity Effects

What we call "opportunity effects" are different in two key ways from the previous effects. First, they are likely not directly associated with mental health outcomes. Second, we are not aware of any hard evidence that shows that these effects actually occur. In essence, "opportunity effects" is a label that captures how clients are seen differently by others because they behave differently due to career development interventions or processes as well as the resulting life, ability, self-perception, and opportunity-perception effects. The now confident, outward-focused, self-managed individual is noticed by others (e.g., educators, supervisors, employers) in a different way than they were prior to career development interventions. This different perception by others can then result in more—and better—work opportunities, learning opportunities, and relationship opportunities.

These opportunities may not directly enhance mental health, but all increase the possibility of significant "life effects" (e.g., better work, more pay, higher status) being accrued. Consider the many clients you have had who entered your service a little dejected, somewhat sour, perhaps sloppily dressed, and complaining that "there are no jobs out there." Even though they made this claim, you patiently helped these clients develop direction, capacity, and self-awareness in the knowledge that there would be "no work out there" for them until *they* changed, but that there was "work out there" for the person who was ready to see the opportunities. This is part of the magic of career practice, and like most magic, it is difficult to operationalize, test, and generate clear-cut evidence for. It is not impossible, however, and we hope that a broad career-development and mental-health research agenda includes this set of effects in its scope.

Summary

According to the Career Development Effects Model we propose in this chapter, career development processes—whether they occur via a formal intervention, self-help resource, life circumstance, or individual's choice—lead to five distinct but connected sets of outcomes or effects: life effects, ability effects, self-perception effects, opportunity-perception effects, and opportunity effects. Each set of effects contributes to, or is a component of, positive mental health. Consider two examples: Work or employment, a life effect, is a well-documented contributor to mental health. Career development competencies, part of the set of ability effects, contribute to environmental mastery, a significant component of mental health.

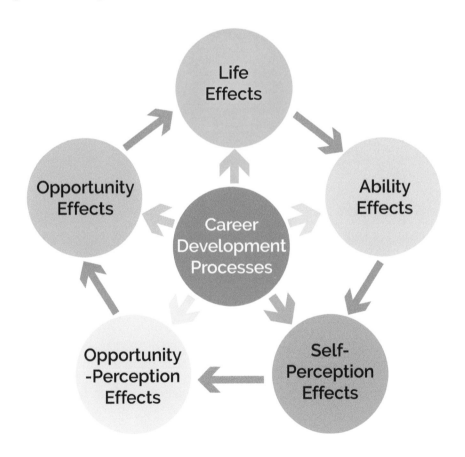

The model portrays career development processes contributing to each set of effects but also recognizes that each set of effects contributes to another, in a sequence, creating a virtuous cycle. For example, seeing oneself as more capable is a self-perception effect that can result from developing career development competence, an ability effect.

The evidence base supporting the effects and their connections to mental health becomes increasingly scarce as one moves through the sequence of effects. There is considerable evidence that career development intervention generates life effects and that these promote mental health outcomes; there is almost no research regarding opportunity effects. There are many gaps in the research that would help the career development field make the case for its contribution to mental health.

Reflection Questions

1. How does your work as a career development practitioner help you create and hold useful self-perceptions and opportunity-perceptions?

2. In what set of effects described in this chapter could you make the most mental health impact in your practice?

3. In what set of effects described in this chapter could you most likely make a noticeable difference with clients or students if you were to engage in further learning? What would this learning entail?

Nothing is either good or bad but thinking makes it so.

William Shakespeare

To Ponder...

Think of a time when you were worried about coping with the demands in your life. Consider the moment when your worry subsided or disappeared. What happened that led to the changes in your perceptions and feelings?

6. Career Development Intervention and Stress

We saw in the previous chapter that career development interventions produce many possible outcomes or effects that are simultaneously mental health outcomes or can influence mental health outcomes. As a result, career development practitioners—regardless of the specific processes, services, or programs they employ—cannot *not* influence mental health outcomes. Given the inevitable myriad of possible career development interventions, how can we collectively understand and enhance the mental health outcomes of our work? Our field has to tackle these interventions one by one—this will be an important research agenda—but what can be done in the meantime? For you as a practitioner, the key is to intentionally adjust the things you are already doing to recognize and amplify existing mental health outcomes (we will return to this topic in Chapters 8 and 9). Then, it is important to examine something that all career development interventions have in common: increasing client capacity for coping, which in turn increases the likelihood of managing stress.

Stress brings us to Shakespeare, quoted above. Shakespeare was at least partially right: Our perceptions about (1) situations and experiences and

(2) our capacity to manage them effectively largely determine what we feel and/or experience in those situations. Career-related demands are among the most important and far-reaching demands people face, and they encompass so much more than "finding a job." The stress caused by the possibility of not coping increases the likelihood of negative mental health outcomes.

We know that feeling stressed is ultimately what brings all clients to a career development practitioner. Clients need help with a specific situation, and they are worried about their ability to manage the situation, and the concomitant stress, on their own. In this chapter, we show the mental health outcomes that naturally emerge from career interventions. Then we describe how to view any career development intervention from the perspective of helping a client perceive that they can manage important demands, thereby reducing stress. Finally, we combine these two efforts to see the interaction between them.

Stress in Action: A Vignette

Robert is 47, married, has two teenage children and has worked for the past 15 years as a project management engineer in the IT department of an oil and gas company. For the second time in his life, he is terminated as a consequence of a downturn in the oil and gas sector. Over the years, he has known many others who have been through job loss, and they usually found a similar placement shortly thereafter. He is worried, but not very. He receives nine months' severance pay and a career support package with a national outplacement agency. Owing to his experience, seniority, and productivity track record, he is reasonably confident about finding a new place in the industry.

Robert starts applying for positions immediately and continuously. Ten months later, with no economic improvement in the industry and only three interviews under his belt, Robert is becoming increasingly worried. Although the family has reduced expenses, financial demands are accumulating rapidly. Robert feels increasing shame, discouragement, and stress. He is losing hope of finding work. At his physician's recommendation, he starts treatment for anxiety and depression. His physician also recommends support, so Robert books a meeting with the outplacement counsellor, a career development practitioner.

Eleven months after his termination, Robert embarks on a career development intervention that has him take detailed stock of his history and credentials along with his interests, values, specialized skills, transferable skills, and natural abilities. He looks at life roles and develops prioritized goals for different parts of his life. His perspective begins to shift. Over the six weeks of mostly regular meetings with his career development practitioner, Robert starts to feel more confident and hopeful, not only about returning to work, but about finding meaningful work in areas he had not previously considered. Robert now sees work as one important part of his life but not the most important part. He begins to understand how he will be okay if he does not return to the oil and gas industry. With freshly sharpened interview skills and a job search portfolio that emphasizes his transferable skills and project management outcomes, he is confident about finding a place in a different industry. He knows the jobs are there, knows his competencies would add value, and feels confident about communicating his value in the job search process.

Three months after meeting with the career development practitioner, Robert accepts a position as team lead with the IT department at a local post-secondary education institution. Robert feels reasonably confident about the fit of the new position, but he also feels he would be able to cope if he needed to engage in the search process again. He also has the sense that he is putting more of himself into, and enjoying more deeply, the other parts of his life. He feels markedly less stressed and ends treatment for depression and anxiety.

Robert's story illustrates the relationships between demands, perceptions of coping, and mental health. As you read it, you were no doubt reminded of your own experience with stress as well as the experiences of many of the clients you have worked with over the years. You have probably learned along the way that stress is central to the human experience, that without it we would be dead (Selye, 1973). Being alive and responding to the demands of life entails experiencing some level of stress. This idea has been captured in the popular self-help movement as the "joy" of stress and in the popular stress/arousal/performance research of Yerkes and Dodson (1908), whose timeless law states that there is an optimal level of arousal for best performance. Yerkes and Dodson remind us that stress has both an upside and a downside. The upside is that we experience stress when we are pursuing our passions, working toward an outcome that we care about, encountering and overcoming challenges along the way, and persevering through setbacks to achieve the desired outcome. The downside of stress refers both to the ways that high stress levels can actually prevent us from performing at our best and achieving the goals we have set for ourselves, and to the outcomes associated with long-term exposure to excessive stress. These outcomes include the personal and life consequences of burnout and the negative physical and mental health effects known to be associated with stress.

What Is Stress?

What do people mean when they speak of "stress"? Defining stress is difficult, even for the experts. In the research literature, stress can be framed as a stimulus (the cause), a response (the reaction), the interaction of stimulus, response, and contextual factors, and the pure interaction of the stimulus and the response (Greenberg, 2013). For our purposes, the following combined definition is useful: For human beings, stress is a composite response to external or internal demands.

The stress response includes physiological, cognitive, and behavioural elements or reactions. In its extreme form, when an organism prepares itself to address an external threat, the stress response is popularly known as the fight or flight response. Perception of a threat triggers a cascading series of hormonal responses that prepare the muscles to take action to address the threat. Icons of this response include prey such as a gazelle or zebra suddenly becoming aware of and responding to the imminent pounce of a hungry predatory lion. You have experienced it yourself if you have ever been chased by a barnyard animal or a snarling dog. Your body responded immediately to the threat and took action— to run from, say, the hissing goose only to trip and fall to the ground, hands pressed firmly to some fresh goose droppings, heart pounding. Or, if you didn't move, your body still responded to your awareness of the threat and to the immediate hormonal gush: a pounding heart, feeling lightheaded, and perhaps confusion about how to best respond to the situation. We are all familiar with the fight or flight response because our bodies are "wired" to do this. Features of the fight or flight response includes the following:

- Elevated heart rate and breathing
- Inhibition of stomach and upper intestinal activity with the slowing of digestion
- Constriction of peripheral blood vessels and dilation of the vessels feeding the muscles
- Activation of stored energy sources, especially fat and glycogen
- Visual (tunnel vision) and auditory (reduced acuity) effects

Many other bodily and brain impacts stem from the stress response. It is interesting to realize that our bodies also respond to threats that are much smaller, less obvious, and seemingly less disruptive. Our point in describing the extreme, or acute, reaction is to provide a clear example of the stress response. The point of all stress-related physiological changes is to prepare the body to take physical action.

Encounters with wild animals or crazed dogs are not the most common threats or stressors currently faced by human beings. Our biggest stressors are the demands imposed by our modern-day existence. The threats stem from our conceptions about what it means to survive and live well in the world. These conceptions or meanings vary from person to person and are largely shaped by one's culture. Culture shapes the meaning of threats, the experience for the individual, and the eventual treatment of individuals facing the threats (Gurung & Roethel-Wendorf, 2009). The experience of stress varies from person to person, but concerns about money, relationships, employment (or lack thereof), traumas, losses, and many other experiences are prevalent, and all require some kind of a response to address a perceived threat.

As you probably know, stress can play a part in the development of many medical conditions, such as hypertension, stroke, cardiovascular disease, ulcers, migraine and tension headaches, allergies and asthma, arthritis, back pain, and obesity, (Greenberg, 2013), as well as mental health concerns and mental illness conditions such as depression and anxiety. Those maladies are but a few known to be linked to stress in some way. Your work as a career development practitioner helps your clients to cope better. Better coping results in reduced stress. Reduced stress, in turn, lowers the chances of the various medical problems associated with stress.

Early understandings of stress tended to view it as a response to a threat in the external environment. Walter Cannon's (1929) early work on the fight or flight response in animals exemplifies this idea, as does Hans Selye's work, which viewed human stress as "the body's non-specific response to any demand made upon it" (Selye, 1973, p. 692). Selye's work honoured the idea that demands could be positive or negative, challenge or threat, and that the body would respond in some way to the demands placed on it. Selye referred to positive stress or stress arising from positive challenges as *eustress* and stress arising from negative events or challenges as *distress*. Selye's work led to an increased awareness of the deleterious effects of negative stress and ultimately set the stage for a stress-research industry seeking to better understand and to intervene with stress.

An offshoot of Selye's work was the development of the Life Events Stress Scale (Holmes & Rahe, 1967), which saw external events or demands as primary sources of stress. Physicians Holmes and Rahe were well aware of the medical consequences of stress. Their scale's development emerged from the idea that individuals experiencing more major life events (e.g., moving, divorce, death, job loss) in the recent past would be more likely to experience a medical illness. In this case, stress was predicted by the number of major life events the individual had recently experienced. Events on the scale ranged in their capacity to elicit stress. A higher score meant one had recently experienced a greater number of significant life events, more-impactful life events, or both, and indicated a greater susceptibility to medical illness. In fact, research has validated Holmes and Rahe's model: There is a predictive relationship between major life events and medical illness (Noone, 2017). Individuals experiencing more major life events tend also to experience more medical illness.

Each of the researchers mentioned above contributed an important piece to the overall understanding of stress. It was Lazarus and Folkman's (1984) work, however, that explained how individuals can experience the same life events differently. Different levels of stress result from these different experiences, and different consequences ensue.

The Transactional Model of Stress and Coping

According to the transactional model of stress and coping, an individual's experience of stress is a product of their perceptions about coping with the important demands they are facing. The model is useful in considering and framing interventions to reduce or avoid stress and for understanding coping and coping strategies that can be implemented to reduce stress.

In the transactional model, stress stems from an individual's interaction with their environment. The individual perceives an environmental demand and simultaneously assesses (appraises) his or her capacity for managing, or coping with, that demand. Events thought to be more demanding, more important, and for which one is less prepared to cope produce more stress for the individual. Conversely, if the demand is perceived as either irrelevant or easily coped with, excessive stress is averted.

Let us take a moment to define the main terms in the model:

- *Demands* are circumstances in the individual's external or internal environment that may require a response.
- *Coping* is "engaging in behavior or thought to respond to a demand" (Greenberg, 2013, p. 110).
  - Task-oriented coping: taking action that addresses the demand directly
  - Emotion-focused coping: managing one's emotional reaction or focusing on acceptance of the situation
- *Appraisal* is the individual's assessment of the demand(s) of a situation and their capacity for coping. *Reappraisal* determines if further coping effort is required once coping has been attempted.
  - *Primary appraisal* determines the relevance and size of the demand(s). Primary appraisal might include asking "Is this important?" and "Is this a threat to my wellbeing or future?"
  - *Secondary appraisal* determines the resources one has to meet the demand(s). Secondary appraisal might include questions such as "How prepared am I to cope with the demand?"

As an example, consider delivering a new workshop that you have developed. Your primary appraisal might lead to thoughts such as, "I've put a lot of effort into developing this; I hope it goes well" and "If this doesn't go well, my boss will be some upset!" As you go through a secondary appraisal, your internal dialogue might include "I've delivered a lot of workshops, but none where I have to be as quick on my feet as this one" or "I'm not sure I'll be able to connect with this client group."

Primary appraisal (assessment of the demand) includes three elements:

- **Goal relevance**. What does the demand mean for the individual? Does the demand relate to things they care deeply about? Relevant goals are more important.

- **Goal congruence/incongruence**. How will dealing with the demand impact the individual's goals? Does the demand support or interfere with those goals? Demands related to goals are more important.

- **Type of ego-involvement**. How closely are the demand and coping with it related to the individual's identity or sense of self?

Secondary appraisal (assessment of coping) also includes three elements:

- **Blame or credit**. Who is responsible for managing this demand? Is it the individual or someone else?

- **Coping potential**. Can the individual manage this situation in a way that addresses the threat or produces the outcome they want?

- **Future expectations**. Is coping with this demand important to the individual's future (goal congruence)?

As you can see, there are some nuances to the appraisal that account for the individual's development (e.g., culture, values, goals, modelling, learning) and their personal attributes or competencies for coping. But, if we step back from the details here, you will notice that no two individuals will appraise the meaning of a demand the same way, nor will they bring the same capacity to coping with it.

A Framework for Stress Control

A useful application and extension of Lazarus and Folkman's work is found in Bryan Hiebert's Framework for Stress Control (Hiebert, 1988; see Figure 6.1). This application extends the model to include decisions about intervention—about how to help clients better control their stress. Of note, this model provides opportunities for intervention both at the level of the demand, or stressor, and by focusing on the stress response itself.

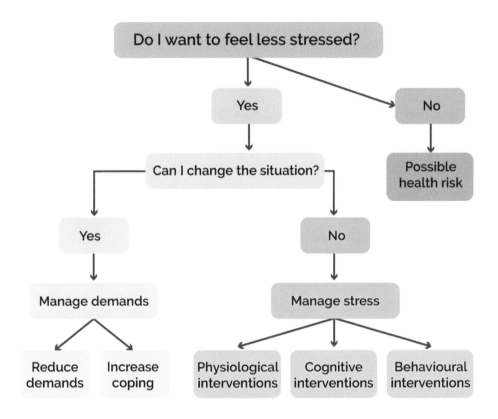

Figure 6.1. **Framework for stress control.** From "Controlling Stress: A Conceptual Update," by B. Hiebert, 1988, *Canadian Journal of Counselling and Psychotherapy, 22*(4), p. 231.

Hiebert's framework is akin to a decision tree and begins with the question "Do I want to feel less stressed"? If the answer is "No"—as it can be for people in circumstances where stress is highly desirable (e.g., high-performance athletes)—then life carries on and the individual is set to experience the consequences, big or small, positive or negative, of resulting stress. If the answer is "Yes," then decisions can be made about how best to intervene. The next question is, "Can I change the situation?" Answering "Yes" leads to options for stressor management, that is, dealing proactively with the source of stress. Overall, dealing with the source of stress (task-oriented coping) has been shown to be the most effective stress-intervention strategy (Epstein, 2011). The two options and key questions for managing a stressor are as follows:

1. **Reduce demands**. "Is it possible to reduce the demands?" Demands are additive, and reducing or eliminating some can immediately cause an individual to perceive that it is now possible to cope with the remaining demands.[10] Classic examples of reducing demands include such things as getting an extension on a project or assignment, reducing work or volunteer commitments, or getting help with demands that exceed one's capacity. In all of these examples, it is the demand that changes, and the change restores the imbalance between the demand and the coping. If it is not possible to reduce the demands, the next order of intervention addresses coping itself.

2. **Increase coping capacity**. The question here is, "Is there anything I can do to cope more effectively with the demands I'm facing?" This level of intervention is usually about learning to better cope with the demands. A person with financial worries, for example, might need better budgeting skills. People facing new demands at work (e.g., writing, public speaking), might bolster, or plan to bolster, their skills through relevant training. Increased coping capacity doesn't alter a demand, but it does change perceptions about one's ability to cope and ought to help ultimately with managing the demand.

---

[10] Note that reducing demands currently may lead to new demands, more stress, and other complications in the future. Dropping a course, for example, may provide immediate stress relief, but at what cost? It may mean taking a summer course, not being able to work in the summer, not having enough money to go to school the following fall, and perhaps, as comedian Chris Farley's fictional motivational speaker Matt Foley was fond of saying, living the rest of your life in a van by the river because you did not complete your education!

If the answer to "Can I change the situation?" is "No," Hiebert's framework provides three options for addressing the physiological, cognitive, and behavioural components of stress, respectively:

1. **Become physiologically less stressed.** "What can I do to adjust my physiological response?" We could get into the weeds with this area alone because there is so much evidence about the kinds of things we can do to feel more relaxed (see for example Park, 2013; Varvogli & Darviri, 2011). Such interventions include the fundamentals of getting enough rest, eating properly, and exercising, as well as the trained-up relaxation approaches of yoga, meditation, relaxation training, and Tai Chi, for example. Many of these are the kinds of things a relative or friend might advise you to do if you were feeling overly stressed. All of these approaches work over time and with repetition to reduce the extent of the body's stress response.

2. **Adjust cognition or thinking**. "How can I adjust my thinking so that I experience less stress?" This level of intervention refers to both primary and secondary appraisal: thinking in a way that changes one's perception about the demands they are facing and/or their ability to cope with it. To these ends, one might focus on how the demand is not actually as important or critical as they thought it was, or how they are in fact quite prepared to cope because they have done so when faced with similar demands in the past.

3. **Behave as if coping is happening**. This level of intervention taps into the powerful, predictive effect of "acting as if." Acting angry or raising one's voice, for example, tends to increase angry thoughts and feelings. The same is true of stress. Working furiously, panicking, or behaving as if a catastrophe is happening can actually increase the physiology and cognition of stress. This intervention category invites the person to slow down.

Hiebert's framework provides a line of questioning you can use with clients that starts with the "lowest hanging fruit." First, you might ask if any of the demands they are facing could be reduced or eliminated. Usually there a few options for doing so. Second, you would explore with clients what they can do to cope more effectively with the demands they are facing. As mentioned above, this part of the intervention is about finding skills that our client could learn to correct the imbalance between demands and coping. It is important to note that the positive impact of any intervention is felt *as soon as the individual perceives the possibility of a better balance between demands and coping.* For example, a student will feel less stressed the moment they decide to drop a course, or reduce their work or volunteer hours, or attend a study-skills workshop. Why? Because they can now appraise the imbalance between the demand and coping in favour of coping.

If it is not possible to reduce demands or increase coping, or if the individual prefers not to do either, then the next step is to address the physiological, cognitive, and behavioural aspects of the stress response. There is an evidence base for approaches in these areas, and over time—and with practice—they can have a marked positive impact on stress experience.

Applying the Framework for Stress Control to Career Development Intervention

Given you are reading this book, you probably have a sense of where we go now. We will draw on an extended application of Hiebert's framework by Huston and Dobbs (2014) to explain how career development intervention is usually a stress management intervention (Did you know you did stress intervention in your role as a career development practitioner?), and thereby also a mental health intervention. In this case, the authors have paralleled Hiebert's stress management framework, but have started with the question "Am I experiencing career-related stress?" (see Figure 6.2).

For our purposes, individuals experience career-related stress when they perceive (appraise) that they may not be able to cope with the career-related demands they are facing; that the demands exceed their coping resources. Career-related demands are represented by a range of concerns, such as "What am I going to study?", "How can I hope, in this economy, to find work that will sufficiently support me and my family?", "What will I do in retirement?", and many others.

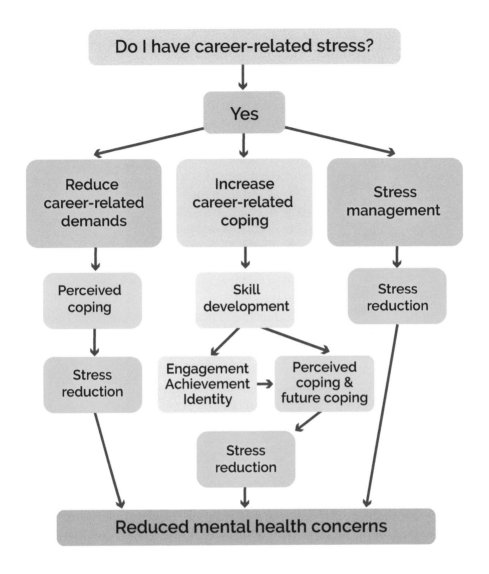

Figure 6.2. **Career development intervention as mental health intervention.** Adapted from "Making the case for career development as a mental health intervention: A literature review with some interesting findings," by M. Huston & J. Dobbs (2014). Paper presented at the Annual Conference of the Canadian Association of College and University Student Services, Halifax, Nova Scotia, Canada.

As per Hiebert's framework, individuals experiencing stress should first try to deal with the source of their stress. When applied to career-related stress, these options are as follows:

1. **Reduce demands (not only career-related demands).** Notice here that we suggest reducing "demands" rather than "career-related demands" specifically. This is because, as stated above, demands are additive and reducing *any* demands can positively change the imbalance between demands and coping resources. Any demand that can reasonably be let go may free up resources to cope with the demands that remain. We can also reduce self-imposed demands. For example, as a career development practitioner, it is possible to reduce career demands by validating and normalizing a client's perceptions. Consider students whose expectations to "know" what they will do or become are compounded by messages from peers, parents, popular media, and by the social, economic, and political environment in which they live. These students are often relieved to learn that there is nothing terribly wrong with them, but that they are part of the majority and completely normal. The demand dissipates, and stress is significantly averted. Much of your work as a career development practitioner helps clients reduce tangible external demands or self-imposed or other-imposed internal demands, such as high personal or familial expectations.

2. **Increase coping resources (not only career-related resources).** Do you ever encourage or support your clients to cope better with non-career-related demands? As noted above, and as you probably know from your own experience, demands are additive. If you help your clients to cope more effectively with *any* of the demands they are facing, they are likely to experience less stress. Career development practitioners usually provide such support to their clients in the form of skill-building, such as learning about career decision-making, writing a resumé, or learning interview skills and the like. This is the domain in which career development practitioners work and thrive. As we discussed in Chapter 5, skill-building is likely to increase competencies (ability effects), and with them personal factors such as self-acceptance, identity, commitment, self-efficacy, confidence, and many others (self-perception effects). All these changes support or increase an attitudinal state that favours

coping efforts and increases the positive appraisal of one's coping resources for managing the career-related demands. This positive appraisal of one's capacity to cope reduces stress and thereby bolsters mental health. In our model (Figure 6.2), all three categories of intervention—reduce demands, increase coping resources, manage stress—reduce stress, but building coping capacity through skill development leads to additional important outcomes, including achievement in other areas such as academic work and being more engaged in school and/or work. Building coping capacity also leads to improved future coping as individuals repeatedly encounter career concerns over the lifespan (Huston & Dobbs, 2014).

Career development practitioners achieve considerable gains with clients, including stress reduction, by focusing on these two areas: reducing demands and increasing coping. Addressing the stress response itself and helping clients to manage stress may not be necessary and may not be within your range of competencies (more on that in the next chapter).

3. **Manage stress.** The stress management options applied to career-related stress are as follows:

   - **Become physiologically less stressed.** Eat better, get sleep and exercise, and learn to relax (e.g., yoga, meditation, relaxation training, mindfulness, exercise).

   - **Adjust thinking about self and demands (e.g., more realistic, gentle, forgiving).** Can demands and coping be appraised in a gentler way? As part of your helping skills and working relationship with your clients, you no doubt naturally contribute to this level of intervention. You have helped your clients to adjust their thinking about their demands and their skills for coping with them, and they have likely felt less stressed as a result.

   - **Act as if coping is happening or "behave better."** Some portion of this category is also part of career development practitioner's repertoire. If you have ever helped a client with their handshake, or arriving on time, or dressing to fit the environment, and countless other behaviour adjustments, then you have been helping them to act as if they are coping. And, as above, they likely felt less stressed as a result.

In this adaptation of Hiebert's intervention model, career development intervention is viewed as a mental health intervention due to its function in reducing the stress clients experience. The stress reduction is accomplished primarily by helping clients to cope more effectively with career-related demands.

A Combined Model

We know that helping your clients to address stress supports their positive mental health. However, career development intervention contributes more to mental health than stress management. To show this we draw on the Career Development Effects Model discussed in Chapter 5 and the evidence base supporting it. To remind you, the five sets of effects in this model are as follows:

- *Life effects:* the impact of career development on an individual's life
- *Ability effects:* the skills, knowledge, and attitudes (competencies) acquired through career development processes as well as life effects
- *Self-perception effects:* the ways individuals see themselves differently due to career development processes as well as life effects and/or ability effects
- *Opportunity-perception effects:* the ways individuals see the world and the opportunities in it differently due to career development processes, life effects, ability effects, and/or self-perception effects
- *Opportunity effects:* the ways opportunities become available to individuals due to career development processes, life effects, ability effects, self-perception effects, and/or opportunity-perception effects

Figure 6.3 integrates these career development effects with the model of transactional stress and coping discussed earlier. It shows how career development intervention produces both stress reduction and career development effects, along with some of the mechanisms linking career development intervention and mental health outcomes.

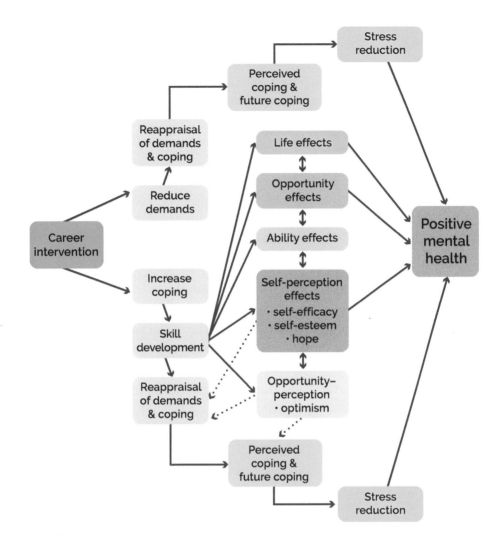

Figure 6.3. Combined career development effects and transactional stress and coping model.

Noteworthy features of the combined model, all of which contribute to positive mental health, include the following:

- **Demand reduction.** Career development intervention can reduce demands, resolving the perceived imbalance between demands and coping resources. This process reduces stress and, in so doing, contributes to positive mental health.

- **Increased coping**. Career development intervention, at its best, leads to skill development or the establishment of new short- and long-term coping skills. Coping skills also contribute to resolving the perceived imbalance between demands and coping resources, thereby reducing stress and, in turn, contributing to positive mental health.

- **Ability effects**. Career development intervention can lead to the development of coping skills, or skills managing career-related and other important demands.

- **Self-perception effects.** Having skills and competencies (ability effects) contributes to the reappraisal of demands and coping resources in terms of recognizing one's capacity to manage important demands, thereby reducing stress. Ability effects such as improved self-efficacy, self-esteem, and sense of purpose all contribute to positive mental health.

- **Life effects**. Career development intervention can lead to work and/or meaningful participation in the social world and to an increased sense of social contribution, environmental mastery, and, thereby, positive mental health.

- **Hope**. That career development intervention produces hope is well-documented. If hope is about perceptions of coping projected over the long term, then it is related to positive mental health.

In all, this combined model shows how career development intervention supports positive mental health both by its function as an intervention for stress and through the development of skills and competencies supporting career development ability, self-perception, opportunity-perception effects, opportunities, and ultimately life effects. All of these contribute to positive perceptions of coping and to factors directly related to positive mental health.

Summary

Understanding stress and coping contributes to the understanding of the mechanisms by which career development intervention supports positive mental health. Stress is a normal physiological, cognitive, and behavioural response to the demands one faces and one's efforts to cope with them. It is exacerbated by perceptions that (1) coping is important or even critical, (2) there is uncertainty about how to cope, and (3) there is uncertainty about whether or not coping efforts will work.

Stress can be addressed at the level of the stressor (demand) or by focusing on the stress reaction. Stressors are addressed by either reducing or eliminating the demand or increasing one's ability to cope, usually by acquiring skills to manage the demand presently and in the future.

Career concerns are among the most important and stress-inducing demands individuals face. Career development intervention can assist its recipients to understand these important demands, reduce them in some cases, and, most importantly, develop skills and competencies to cope with them. Stress is mitigated as soon as the individual perceives they will be able to cope with their most important demands, career and otherwise. Career development intervention leads both to immediate perceptions of current and future coping and to actual coping. It is this function of career development intervention that contributes to stress mitigation, reduction, and elimination and to the associated positive mental health benefits. The skill development and related outcomes or effects associated with career development intervention also produce life circumstances, attitudes, and mindsets that are either consistent with, or included in, current understandings and definitions of mental health.

Reflection Questions

1. How can you apply the transactional model of stress and coping in your own life to better manage your demands and your experience of stress?

2. How can the combined career development effects and transactional stress and coping model be implemented easily and immediately with your current clients?

3. What work- and role-related skills can you learn to better cope with the most significant demands you face in your role as a career development practitioner?

What you do makes a difference, and you have to decide what kind of difference you want to make.

Jane Goodall

To Ponder...

Consider your role as a career development practitioner and the value of your work for enhancing the wellbeing and mental health of your clients. What ethical concerns or issues come to mind?

7. The Role of the Career Development Practitioner with Respect to Mental Health: Ethical Implications

In this chapter, we discuss the ethical implications and considerations career development practitioners face as they practice with mental health awareness. To immediately allay any concerns you may have, let us assure you that nothing fundamental has changed; you will continue to do your work as before with the provision that you now understand the relationship between career development intervention and positive mental health outcomes. There are no new ethical implications associated with practicing career development intervention with mental health awareness. That's right—no new ethical implications!

To get us in the right mindset, we begin with a vignette set in a Canadian post-secondary educational institution.

Simji is a career development practitioner at a small university in British Columbia. John has moved to British Columbia from Calgary, Alberta, to start his first year of a BSc in Forest Ecology and Management. He starts working with Simji two months into the school year, when he is referred to career services by a social worker he had met with twice. His motivation to pursue a career path in forestry has diminished to nothing and he is increasingly worried that he has made a terrible mistake. He is consumed by thoughts of the money he is potentially wasting and the financial problems and cost he is creating for his parents.

The social worker helps John understand stress and identify some of the key demands he is facing. Although he is slightly homesick, he likes the adventure of living in a new place and is gradually becoming involved in the community and developing some friendships. He is concerned about his grades, but by far his biggest worry is about having made a terrible decision that could possibly ruin his life.

Simji and John meet for career support three times over two weeks. Simji leads John through a career development process that helps him to gather and organize information about himself (e.g., interests, values, skills, needs) and the world of possibilities for schooling and work (e.g., types of institutions, degrees, majors, minors, occupations, jobs) and to learn about career development, career decision-making, and life-role career planning. She also validates and normalizes John's concerns, helping him to understand that by being undecided he is actually part of the majority of first-year students on campus. By the third meeting with Simji, John has not made any decisions, but he is feeling confident about what he needs to do to move forward with his career decision-making process. He tells Simji that things are much better: His worry about having made a terrible mistake has disappeared, he is studying well again, and he knows he is going to be okay even if he decides to study something other than forestry, which he is re-understanding as fitting with some of his interests and values.

Simji is pleased for John and equally pleased with the immediate, positive feedback about client outcomes. At lunch, she recounts the story to her co-worker, noting she is happy that her work has made such a positive difference for her client's mental health. Her colleague cautions her not to talk too much about "positive mental health outcomes" with the team or in the department. "We don't want them thinking we're doing mental health intervention over here." Simji is aware of the career development-mental health boundary at her institution and agrees about the problems or, at minimum, the discussion that would ensue if she made any claims about the mental health benefits of her work. Until this point, she has felt positive about her work with John. Now she feels a bit ashamed, wondering if she has done something wrong and should have handled things differently.

The Implications of Intentionality

Earlier in the book, we discussed the fear that you and many career development practitioners might have about providing a service that influences mental health. Remember: Whether you know it, plan it, or want it, your career development services inevitably create and influence mental health outcomes. We hope that in reading our book you now know this and know that there is evidence to support it; you now know that career development intervention works to bolster overall wellbeing and mental health.

So, how did you answer our "To Ponder…" question above? Our experience with the topic is that it evokes a visceral reaction of worry accompanied by a concern that it is possible, or even easy, to have an ethical lapse when intervening with clients in a way that supports positive mental health outcomes. If, whether you intend it or not, doing your work as you always have creates mental health outcomes, why are you concerned about the ethics of it all? This is neither a dismissive nor rhetorical question. We think there are a few important reasons for reactions of worry and concern:

- You identify as a career development practitioner responsible for creating career development outcomes. Although you have probably been aware of mental health outcomes, you have not identified as a practitioner whose work supports positive mental health.

- You have been careful in all your work not to dabble in "personal counselling"; you have steered your clients away from talking about their personal concerns. Somewhere along your career path you learned to think about your work solely for its relationship to work-related career development outcomes. Perhaps you have read about or heard an expert discuss how it is critical to not blend the two.

- Your employer reminds you of the clear separation between your role and responsibilities as a career development practitioner and those of a mental health practitioner. This can happen especially in organizations providing both services, such as post-secondary educational institutions or schools.

- Your profession has not emphasized the mental health benefits of career development intervention, and in your training and experience over the years you have not been encouraged or provided instruction about how to integrate mental health outcomes.

- You know that you are not qualified to intervene in mental illness issues. You experience an emotional resistance to working with mental health outcomes, even though you can conceptually distinguish mental illness and mental health.

Career development practitioners like you have long worked with the idea that intervention with mental health is best left to those professionals who specialize in the area. And, of course, we agree completely that career development practitioners should work within the boundaries of their competence. Given what we now know about the benefits of career development intervention for personal wellbeing, we wondered if there was a way to work within our professional boundaries, continuing to perform our best career work, but with an understanding of how it benefits mental health and wellbeing. We also reflected on the value of sharing this understanding with clients and other key stakeholders. We think it is possible to be intentional about mental health in career development practice, and this is why we devote a chapter to the ethical implications of understanding career development intervention broadly as mental health and wellbeing intervention.

The basics of your work—the fundamental things you do to help clients manage career demands—will continue as it did before you became intentional about mental health outcomes in your practice. Understanding these other benefits of your work, however, reveals opportunities to share that information with clients and other stakeholders. Mental health/illness concerns are common. As a career development practitioner, you have certainly provided career development services to clients experiencing mental health concerns and mental illness conditions, and while your services have helped those clients address their career concerns, their mental health and wellbeing have benefited as well. Wellbeing and mental health benefits are common and have always happened in career development practice. It is your intentionality around these outcomes and your commitment to sharing the evidence with your clients and stakeholders that is new.

Applying Ethical Principles to Mental Health Awareness in Career Development Intervention

An important accepted element in the discussion of ethics is that career development practitioners are expected to behave ethically. This expectation is consistent among all the professional associations and/or governing bodies that have either developed or adopted a code of conduct for its members (see sidebar: "Codes of Ethics for Career Development Practitioners"). Each of these ethical codes are comprehensive and address ethical issues related to all parts of a career development practitioner's work and behaviour. In this section, we review selected principles in three areas: (1) competency and conduct, (2) the relationship between career development practitioners and clients, and (3) the relationships between career development practitioners and other professionals. Although not exhaustive, the principles reviewed here are both common to all codes and most relevant to working with an awareness of mental health outcomes.

Codes of Ethics for Career Development Practitioners

- Australia: Career Industry Council of Australia (CICA) https://cica.org.au/professional-standards/
- Canada: Canadian Standards & Guidelines for Career Development Practitioners https://career-dev-guidelines.org the-standards-guidelines/code-of-ethics/
- International Association of Educational and Vocational Guidance (IAEVG) https://iaevg.com/Resources - Ethical_S
- United Kingdom: Career Development Institute https://www.thecdi.net/Code-of-Ethics
- United States: National Career Development Association (NCDA) https://www.ncda.org/aws/NCDA/pt/sp/guidelines

Competency and Conduct

Knowledge, Skills, and Competency

Our field is committed to a high standard of service. As a career development practitioner, you understand the importance of knowing about the relationship between your work and wellbeing outcomes. You are competent in your knowledge of the current evidence about the relationship between career development and mental health and can competently use your career development practitioner skills to support your clients as you always have. As we mentioned above, what has changed is your understanding of the extended impact of your work to create mental health outcomes. If the field is going to include mental health impact among the outcomes of career development work, career development practitioners are implicated in knowing the career development–mental health evidence, having a basic understanding of mental health, and having the skills to effectively share that understanding with clients and other stakeholders.

Self-improvement

A commitment to self-improvement means that practitioners are active in maintaining the currency of their knowledge and practice competencies. As new evidence becomes available, career development practitioners are committed to considering it, learning about it, and potentially integrating it in their regular work with clients. We are reasonably confident that the evidence base regarding career development and mental health will expand and become increasingly rigorous over the next few years. We anticipate being able refer to this evidence to support the claims you can make about your role in mental health support. This ethical guideline directs all practitioners to be vigilantly aware of the current evidence and practices and, where possible, to integrate them in their regular work.

Boundary of Competency

Ethical principles about boundaries of competence ask career development practitioners to focus on what they know and do best. In considering your role in mental health support, these ethical principles usually stand out from the rest. Remember the fear you may have felt at the idea of being responsible in some way for mental health outcomes. That fear might have initially been rooted in the linguistic confusion discussed earlier in the book—perhaps you heard "mental illness" instead of "mental health." Or perhaps its source is any of the reasons discussed earlier in this chapter. In any case, most career development practitioners have a clear professional boundary demarcating intervention with career development and intervention with mental health and illness. When working with clients with mental health/illness concerns, practitioners are clear that their focus is on career development, and that mental health/illness concerns are properly the domain of the health care professionals (e.g., doctors, nurses, psychologists, social workers) with whom the client is already engaged. If there are no other professionals working with the client, then practitioners make an appropriate referral to ensure the client is supported.

Practitioners armed with the new understanding and knowledge of career development intervention as a contributor to mental health will continue to do their best career work but will find occasions in which it makes sense to share that knowledge. Practitioners will talk about the potential wellbeing outcomes of their work with clients and stakeholders and be able to do so ethically. (In the following two chapters, we describe practical principles and interpersonal skills that will allow you to do this.)

Marketing

Related to the career development practitioner's role in mental health support, marketing principles refer to how the field communicates publicly with clients and other stakeholders. As we have described, there is a rigorous and expanding base of evidence endorsing career development and career development intervention as a support for mental health. Integrity to the data means career development practitioners are responsible for knowing the meaning of career development intervention research, including its limitations, and sharing it openly and transparently. Additionally, the data will no doubt show that trained, competent career development practitioners can, *within the normal scope of their work, bring about significant mental health outcomes for clients.* It is important that credentials, competence, training, and experience are accurately represented. For example, a website for an employment program could reasonably list the main mental health benefits of employment, particularly employment that "fits" the individual. It could also ethically note the mental health advantages associated with enhancing career development competencies, if enhancing these competencies is part of its service repertoire.

Career Development Practitioner–Client Relationship

Integrity, Honesty, and Objectivity

Behaving with integrity, honesty, and objectivity means that practitioners are accountable for providing accurate information to clients. For our purposes, one can imagine being responsible for knowing generally about mental health and having some understanding of mental health/illness concerns. (Clearly, this understanding need not be as broad or deep as a mental health practitioner's understanding.) Career development practitioners are also implicated in knowing the research as it becomes available (or at least the major research findings) well enough to communicate it accurately and clearly so that clients can make informed and responsible decisions for themselves. As much as possible, practitioners need to describe reasonably expected outcomes of their interventions. You certainly do not want to be the practitioner who promises that excellent mental health or treatment of mental illness will result from your employment services! Raising false hopes can be more damaging to the client than doing nothing at all.

Inherent in this principle is a need to be aware of one's own values and to understand and accept that clients may have different values. Health is a value and, for most people, it is highly prioritized. But this is not true for all people at all times. Furthermore, it is important to note that no intervention, career- or health-related, is completely risk-free. Practitioners need to accurately share unbiased information so that clients and stakeholders can make appropriate decisions.

Confidentiality and Releasing Private Information

Practitioners are responsible for managing and maintaining client confidentiality. Sharing with clients the mental health benefits of career development intervention and, at times, discussing clients' mental health concerns, may have clients sharing rather personal experiences. You likely have already witnessed this in your work. Your ability to develop working alliances and empathize with clients' concerns can have clients rightfully seeing you as a trusted confidante with whom their stories are safely shared. As professionals, practitioners need to be clear about the limits of confidentiality, noting to clients the specific information that cannot remain confidential. It is the practitioner's responsibility to make these areas unambiguously clear to clients and then to verify the client has understood.

Specific language and skills you can use to provide information about confidentiality are described in Chapter 10. We note here that we advocate being clear with clients about your focus on career development, but your openness about the wellbeing outcomes of career development may lead to personal revelations by your clients. This possibility increases your need and responsibility to attend to the principle of confidentiality in a complete way, ensuring clients understand the full meaning of your limit to confidentiality.

Releasing Private Information

Having been clear about the limits of confidentiality and made certain that clients understood the limits, there are then only specific situations in which practitioners have licence to release clients' personal information. It is always best to have the client's permission (preferably written) to release their information to a third party. As with confidentiality, this principle has particular relevance when considering career development and mental health. Practitioners are likely to hear client stories related to mental health/illness as a result of welcoming conversations about wellbeing and sharing information about the mental health benefits of career development work. As with the limits of confidentiality, practitioners need to be clear with clients about the circumstances under which private information can be shared.

Informed Consent

It is your responsibility to inform clients accurately about all aspects of your services, including how information is managed and used, what specific services include and entail, and the expected outcomes and possible limitations of the services. As public awareness expands about the value of career development intervention to positive mental health, we imagine situations in which clients engage in career development intervention or work with a career development practitioner with the intention of bolstering their mental health. This intention is warranted, and the evidence suggests that we can expect wellbeing and mental health benefits accruing to clients who use career services, participate in career development activities, or engage in career development intervention in some other way (e.g., through a work-sponsored career development program). As a service provider, you should be explicit and accurate about the nature of your services and their limitations so that your clients can make an informed, responsible decision about whether or not to participate.

Professional Relationships

Consultation

Consultation with other competent professionals is an important and necessary part of the career development practitioner's work. Referring to mental health and wellbeing benefits stemming from career development interventions will no doubt result in more conversations with clients about mental health and mental illness. Occasionally, because career development practitioners are usually not mental health professionals, they may need additional input, another brain and another set of ears in order to reflect and share expertise about how best to support their clients. Our field is likely to see increasing opportunities for career development practitioners and mental health professionals to work together in meeting the mental health and career development needs of clients. Capacity, licence, and permission to consult will become increasingly important to career development practitioners.

Respect for Other Professionals

Career development practitioners are encouraged to take advantage of other professions' specializations, competence, and relative expertise in meeting the needs of clients. This reinforces the idea that career development practitioners are not responsible for mental health or mental illness intervention; these are properly the domain of other health care professionals. It also allows us to understand how other professionals can appreciate career development's piece of the wellbeing intervention pie.

In the next chapters, we describe practice implications related to career development and mental health. Many of these implications will be directly informed by the ethical principles described above.

Summary

This chapter provided an overview of the ethical principles relevant to recognition of the mental health benefits of career development intervention. Above all, career development practitioners are responsible for maintaining their competence and also expanding their understanding of the evidence base regarding the outcomes of their work. They are responsible for accurate communication with clients and other stakeholders about all aspects of their services, including their limits of competence and their understanding of competencies held by other professionals such as mental health practitioners.

Reflection Questions

1. What services, by your education, professional training, and work experience, are you prepared for and competent to provide for your clients?

2. Consider your role and work as a career development practitioner and the real possibility that your work positively influences mental health and wellbeing. Which ethical principles seem most important and relevant to your work?

3. What services are you sometimes invited to provide that do not fit within the boundaries of your competence or responsibility? How might you better manage this issue in the future?

You cannot hope to build a better world without improving the individuals. To that end, each of us must work for [our] own improvement and, at the same time, share a general responsibility for all humanity, our particular duty being to aid those to whom we think we can be most useful.

Marie Curie

To Ponder...

In your role as a career development practitioner you have certain responsibilities. Regarding mental health and wellbeing, what outcomes are you accountable for that fall within the boundaries of your competence and for which you also have the resources necessary to support you?

8. Practice Implications: Integrating Mental Health Outcomes Within the Career Development Process

We have presented evidence and relevant conceptual models throughout this book to make the case that career development intervention produces positive mental health outcomes. In the previous chapter, we reviewed the ethical principles related to including consideration of mental health outcomes in career development practice. In this chapter, we discuss principles that inform your role and practice with clients. Ethical guidelines point to decisions about how best to behave in and manage specific practice or client situations, providing guidance regarding the rightness or wrongness of decisions. Principles, however, are fundamental or general truths that inform the understanding of an area. Principles are the givens that shape one's approach. In this case, we are referring to principles that are foundational to including consideration of mental health outcomes in your role as a career development practitioner of any stripe—career counsellor, school-based career educator, employment advisor, or career workshop facilitator.

Six Principles for Your Work as a Career Development Practitioner

1. Career development intervention produces career-related effects or outcomes.

   As described in Chapters 5 and 6, career development intervention, the work you do, leads to career development. Career development, in turn, produces outcomes or effects for your clients. We categorized these effects as follows:

   - Life effects
   - Ability effects
   - Self-perception effects
   - Opportunity-perception effects
   - Opportunity effects

2. Career development intervention produces positive mental health outcomes.

   In addition to producing career outcomes, career development intervention addresses stress by either reducing demands or bolstering capacity to cope with demands. Building capacity is usually achieved by the development of competencies for managing demands, which in turn leads to changes in self-perception. The self-perception changes include perceptions of coping now and in the future. Capacity, coping, and perceptions of being able to cope in the future (hope) contribute to positive mental health.

3. The career development practitioner's explicit role in supporting mental health is educational.

   Understanding and accepting Principles 1 and 2 doesn't fundamentally change what you do or how you do it. Your work with clients continues as before, with one exception: You can now help clients and others understand the value of career development processes and interventions in supporting positive mental health. You can assume responsibility for, and take advantage of, opportunities for teaching your clients, as well as colleagues, managers, those in your community, or those in your client's community (e.g., family members, other professionals, caregivers) about the mental health benefits of your work.

4. Career development practitioners are not responsible for assessing or gathering information about clients' mental health concerns or mental illness conditions.

Following from the previous principles, being aware of and focusing on mental health does not implicate career development practitioners in gathering information about clients' mental health concerns or mental illness conditions. It is possible clients will share this and related information within the context of receiving some form of career development intervention. Practitioners might ask for clarification or further information if a mental health concern or illness is mentioned by the client, as it almost certainly will be. When it is mentioned, career development practitioners will have some responsibility for determining the nature and meaning of the information shared and the course(s) of action that might best support the client.

Whatever concerns about mental health/illness clients choose to share, you will continue to work within the boundaries of your competence as a career development practitioner. We talk more about how to do this in the next chapter.

5. The client/practitioner relationship is vitally important to effective career development intervention and must be based on respect, confidentiality, and a focus on career goals.

Clients seeking and/or receiving services from career development practitioners, irrespective of any health concerns, want to be

- respected as persons—viewed as persons first, with unique skills, interest, values, and goals, and not as diagnoses or codes;
- assured of confidentiality and privacy; and

- supported in their focus on career goals rather than being recipients of mental health/illness counselling.

6. Assessment should be for the client's benefit, not the practitioner's.

Career development intervention, at its best, helps clients to learn about themselves, organize their information, and work toward achieving goals they have chosen for themselves in all areas of their lives. Clients want to be assessed for their own benefit, rather than diagnostically, with the goal of more clearly and effectively understanding themselves and their needs.

One of the constraints career development practitioners face in operating in the zone of "best practices" is the unrelenting demand for competent career development services and the seeming requirement during recent economic cycles to do more with less. These constraints sometimes result in system-wide developments in which requisite assessment leads to labelling and/or placement within a service system. In social service and employment contexts, for example, clients are given labels such as "expected to work," "not expected to work," "work or job ready," or "long-term unemployed." It is worth noting that the career development industry is not alone in this. With demand for mental health services at an all-time high, similar quick assessment/placement approaches are implemented there to create service capacity. Given the potential contribution of career development intervention to positive mental health, it makes sense to invest in resources that allow career development practitioners and their clients to use client-centred assessment and the potential mental health benefits and related outcomes it can lead to.

What You Need

With the above principles in mind, we present some of the fundamental competencies career development practitioners probably require in order to integrate an understanding of the mental health benefits of their work into their regular practice.

General Knowledge of Mental Health/Illness

Career development practitioners need general, not necessarily specialized, knowledge of mental health concerns and mental illness conditions and an understanding of the relationship between career development and mental health.

Taking on an educational role related to the mental health benefits of career development will no doubt increase the likelihood of client disclosures of related information. Responsibility for mental health starts with the individual but is shared by schools and post-secondary institutions, workplaces, organizations, and local, regional, and national governments. As with employees and professionals working in other contexts, career development practitioners need a solid general knowledge of mental health and mental illness. We all need this!

Training and Support

Career development practitioners need training and support in managing client disclosures about mental health/illness.

As mentioned above, integrating mental health awareness and sharing information about the mental health benefits of career development will create opportunities for clients to share information about their mental health and illness concerns. Practitioners will need the skills to navigate these conversations while maintaining and working within their boundaries of competence. Training may be necessary, and access to mental health services or resources (or the capacity to refer and consult) will be important to ensure clients who need specialized mental health support are informed of, and guided to, those services.

The Ability to Carry Out Appropriate Assessments

Career development practitioners need to carry out assessments that acknowledge the relationship between mental health and career development while working within their boundaries of competence.

In career development practice, "assessment" can serve the service provider, the client, or both. Mostly, it serves both. Assessment can mean referencing a checklist of client demographic and historical factors to determine eligibility for referral to a specific service or program; gathering general information to determine initial next steps to meet a client's needs; or helping clients to gather, organize, and consider their information and story in order to manage their own development in the future. In each of these meanings or applications, it may be necessary to ask clients about barriers and personal concerns. A normal and common tendency for career development practitioners is to avoid conversations regarding mental health concerns and mental illness conditions. In the last chapter, we referred to the fear you might have at the prospect of being responsible for your clients' mental health. The fear, we think, is normal and a consequence of many things, including training in ethics and the clear, litigation-avoiding boundaries set by employers and organizations.

In order to meet the needs of some of your clients, you need to be able to ask directly about certain experiences and potential barriers, including mental health and illness concerns. However, you need to do this in a way that maintains your boundaries of competence. And this leads directly to the next area of competence.

Communication Skills

Career development practitioners need communication skills that support working within boundaries of competence.

Forms of assessment are but one element in the range of intervention stages and strategies that career development practitioners may provide their clients. Intervention with clients, whether in one meeting or a series of meetings, is navigated from start to finish by communication skills and strategies. In the following chapter, we discuss how intentional use of specific communication skills and techniques can help you to provide effective intervention and share information about the mental health benefits of your work while maintaining the boundaries of your competence as a career development practitioner.

Knowledge of Resources

Career development practitioners need knowledge of mental health/ illness resources.

If you are doing all of the above, you will likely have increasingly in-depth discussions with your clients about mental health and wellbeing. Occasionally, you may become aware of a client who needs the support of competent, specialized mental health resources. Going forward, mental health-aware career development practitioners will be implicated in knowing about the relevant mental health resources available locally, regionally, and online. This knowing can mean different things. In some cases, it is enough to know of a resource, such as an agency or a website, and simply tell your clients about it. But, considering how mental health service providers are struggling more than ever before to meet demands, it can be difficult to link or refer clients to these services. More knowledge about services will help, but the best follow-through on referral stems from a reciprocal relationship with the service and, in the best case, a professional relationship with a specific person who can be contacted.

What You Can Do

Given the tone of the sections above, you are no doubt asking yourself a few questions and waiting patiently for answers. Your questions may include the following, among others:

- How can I integrate awareness of mental health outcomes in my work with clients?
- How do I acknowledge mental health and/or indicators of mental illness while maintaining boundaries of competence?
- How do I maintain confidentiality while making use of (referring to) the mental health resources in our community?

Before we get to the answers, here and in the next chapter, let us remind you again that you are already creating mental health benefits for your clients *by doing what you have always done.* In your role as a career development practitioner, you cannot avoid creating positive mental health outcomes—they are a natural outcome of career development intervention. With this and the above principles and competencies in mind, here are some things you can do without any additional training to amplify the positive mental health benefits of your work:

- **Focus on the relationship.** Listening skills and effective questions can create a place of acceptance for clients to talk about themselves, their concerns, their goals, and their lives.

- **Take time.** Be aware that clients sometimes need more time to feel safe and to trust that you have their best interests at heart. Moreover, stigma is real, and clients may be very hesitant to discuss mental health concerns or mental illness conditions. When you do your best work, there is no substitute for time; what can be accomplished in 10 minutes is not the same as what can be accomplished in 30 minutes. If possible, take more time to listen. (Sometimes, and in some contexts or organizations, this is not possible. We understand that.)

- **Use visual reminders** (posters, pamphlets) of a positive, normalized understanding of mental health and mental health status or symptoms of mental illness.

- **Expand your general knowledge and understanding** of mental health/illness without feeling a need to become an expert.

- **Validate and normalize** client experiences and feelings, thoughts, and behaviours. Your clients have the same general human concerns we all do. They specifically want a job or a career outcome, but you are both concerned about your respective futures. Additionally, all individuals have experienced the impact of mental health concerns, either by evaluating their own mental health or by supporting and observing its impact in the lives of family, friends, or colleagues. Career development practitioners and their clients are more alike than they are different.

- **Treat clients as whole people**, with whole lives they care about; treat them as bigger than their feelings and symptoms.

In the next chapter, we will discuss the interpersonal skills that are relevant to both including mental health awareness in your practice and maintaining your boundaries of competence as a career development practitioner.

Summary

In this chapter, we discussed principles guiding and supporting the inclusion of mental health awareness in your work as a career development practitioner. Principles in this case are the constants in your work that are unlikely to change. Among these constants are some key pieces including: (1) career development produces predictable outcomes, (2) career development along with its associated outcomes produces positive mental health benefits, and (3) despite these mental health benefits, the role of career development practitioners is focused on career development intervention and supporting the whole client. The role of career development practitioners with respect to mental health benefits and outcomes is educational.

Reflection Questions

1. To date, how have you integrated mental health and wellbeing outcomes in your work with clients?

2. Considering your role with clients, which of the principles described in this chapter will be most challenging to honour or implement in your current work environment?

3. Which of the principles described in this chapter present the most opportunity for your own professional development? How could you further your development in this area?

A well-made salad must have a certain uniformity; it should make perfect sense for those ingredients to share a bowl.

Yotam Ottolenghi

To Ponder...

What skills do you use to help your clients understand what will happen in your work together and why it might be important? How do you teach your clients about your role and responsibilities?

9. Use Interpersonal Skills for Mental Health Awareness and Support

Interpersonal skills are specific verbal and non-verbal behaviours that helpers use to support clients in identifying and eventually solving their problems. If you have had any training in communication skills, then some of what we discuss in this chapter will likely be familiar. If you have not studied interpersonal skills, there is still a good chance that you will recognize some of what we discuss because you probably use most of these skills each day, whether you realize it or not. A complete coverage of interpersonal or helping skills is beyond the scope of this book. Instead, we will review the fundamentals and then target a specific set of lesser-known skills that are particularly useful for our purpose, which is to help you make mental health awareness part of your practice. Recall that your role in this regard is primarily educational: to teach your clients about the positive mental health benefits of career development. Fulfilling this role does not require you to add new skills to your repertoire, but rather to apply existing skills intentionally to that end.

There are dozens of different skill sets and/or approaches to using skills in a helping scenario such as a career development intervention. Helping models describe the way that clients enter into, and are facilitated through, the relationship (e.g., Carkuff, 1969; Egan, 2014; Hill, 2014; Ivey, Ivey, & Zalequette, 2010; Martin & Hiebert, 1985). Despite differences in language, terminology, and the exact number of stages or steps, each model provides a process for supporting clients through the same basic, linear sequence:

1. Introduction (beginning) – Determine goals or problem to be solved.
2. Intervention (middle) – Address problem directly or work towards solving the problem.
3. Closure (end) – Evaluate intervention results and plan for the future.

All models also address what specifically the helper will do to facilitate the client through the process, and this includes using interpersonal skills.

To become more intentional about how you use interpersonal skills, it is useful to consider the purpose of different skill sets. A "helping as instruction" model described by Martin and Hiebert (1985) delineates the generic interpersonal skills by function into three discrete categories: questioning, reacting, and structuring.

Questioning Skills

All three skill categories allow you to manage the direction and flow of a helping session, but questions do this best. Questions are used to get the client to do something, to respond by acting or thinking in some way. For our purpose in this chapter—using interpersonal skills to support the positive mental health outcomes of career development intervention—we will discuss two basic categories of questions: closed questions and open questions.

Closed Questions (CQ)

Closed questions (CQ) seek confirmation. By definition, closed questions can be logically answered with a "yes" or "no" and commonly start with words like "is," "are," "do," "have," and so on. Most of us use closed questions frequently in our day-to-day speech, often by habit, and even when a different tool, such as an open question, might better serve our intentions. Appropriate use of closed questions entails asking about something for which yes/no confirmation is needed. For example:

- Did you call your doctor?
- Do you have a resumé?
- Do you have a driver's licence?
- Would it be okay to contact your partner?
- Have you been thinking about suicide?

The response to each of these questions leads to a course of action. Used properly, closed questions can solicit the exact information we need to make a decision about how to proceed. If confirmation is not the aim, a closed question is the wrong tool.

Open Questions (OQ)

In direct contrast to closed questions, open questions (OQ) cannot logically be answered with a "yes" or "no." Accordingly, open questions usually start with words like "what," "how," "when," "where," "why," and "who." The function of open questions is to solicit information from clients. Examples of open questions you likely use regularly include the following:

- What did you like about your last job?
- How long have you been unemployed?
- What is the main thing you would like to accomplish in our meeting today?
- What concerns do you have about starting to look for work?

Appropriate open questions prompt clients to provide information that will help you better understand their needs.

Declarative probes (DPs) are a variant of open questions in which the question is actually a declarative statement. A declarative probe starts with a directive verb such as "tell," "describe," "say," or "think." This questioning skill can be useful with clients who are less talkative than most. Its direct nature makes it more difficult for less-talkative clients to respond with "I don't know" or "nothing." For example:

- Tell me about your work role with Acme.

- Describe your approach to getting ready for an interview.

- Show me how you introduce yourself when you meet a prospective employer.

- Say more about that.

Used intentionally, declarative probes add variety to an interaction while also helping the practitioner to get needed information.

Reacting Skills

Reacting skills function primarily to provide the client feedback about what the practitioner is hearing, seeing, or noticing, so as to create a sense for the client that they are really being listened to. Also, when used with sensitivity, reacting skills help the practitioner check their understanding of the client. The three fundamental verbal reacting skills are paraphrasing, reflecting feeling, and reflecting meaning.

Paraphrasing (PP)

Paraphrasing (PP) is the most commonly used of all the helping skills. By definition, it is a restatement of some portion, using different words, of a client's statement. Again by definition, this means no extra information or inferences are added. Consider the following example:

> **Client**: I'm a bit worried about my future. I'm thinking about majors and I have a few ideas, but I'm really a terrible student. I'm worried I'm going to fail a course or two.
>
> **Practitioner**: You have worries about your future and there are some courses that you're worried you might not pass.

Paraphrases provide feedback and help clients to hear the verbal content of what they are saying. Practitioners might worry that their clients would catch on to and see this as some kind of trick. The truth is, virtually all people are so seldom listened to intentionally that most appreciate paraphrases as a sincere attempt by the listener to understand what they are saying.

Reflecting Feeling (RF)

This skill differs from paraphrasing in that the practitioner makes some inference, based on their client's words, voice, and appearance, about what the client is feeling. Feelings are primary experiences. Accurately expressing in words a client's affective experience not only provides a deep sense for the client of being understood, it can contribute significantly to the client's understanding of their own experience. When reflecting feeling (RF), it is usually more effective to use a feeling word than a metaphor. As well, a "less is more" approach has merit because being more tentative, reflecting without making bold declarations of knowing the client's affective world, allows the practitioner and client room to adjust the reflection for nuance. Consider the following reflections:

> **Client**: I'm a bit worried about my future. I'm thinking about majors and I have a few ideas, but I'm really a terrible student. I'm worried I'm going to fail a course or two.
>
> **Practitioner**: Just listening to how you said that—it sounds like you're feeling a bit inadequate.
>
> **or**
>
> **Practitioner**: It sounds like you're feeling pretty stressed by all of this.

or

> **Practitioner**: Just listening to how you said that—you're worried and you say you're a terrible student, but you seem a teeny bit hopeful.

In each of the examples, the practitioner provides feedback by making an inference. The more we pay attention closely, the better our chances of reflecting accurately the client's affective experience.

Reflecting Meaning (RM)

As with reflections of feeling, reflections of meaning (RM) involve making inferences about the inner life experience of the client. Based on what the client says and does, the practitioner makes inferences about "meaning structures" such as values, interests, preferences, beliefs, personal philosophies, and world view. Meaning structures are affected and determined by many factors including ethnicity, culture, development, family factors, and life experience. No two people are exactly the same in this regard. Meaning is big and all-encompassing, and reflecting it in a close-to-accurate way does much to create the sense of being deeply understood. Given the range of possible meaning structures to make inferences about, actual reflection of meaning can take many forms. Here are a few examples:

> **Client**: I'm a bit worried about my future. I'm thinking about majors and I have a few ideas, but I'm really a terrible student. I'm worried I'm going to fail a course or two.

> **Practitioner**: Just listening to how you said that—it sounds like performing well in school might be important to you. [inference about a value]

> **or**

> **Practitioner**: It seems like you might believe you're not really capable of doing well in school. [inference about a belief]

> **or**

> **Practitioner**: Just listening to how you said that—you would probably prefer to take a few courses you can pass rather than being overloaded. [inference about preference]

The practitioner made an inference about client meaning in each of these cases. It is clear the statements are inferences because the client did not state the meaning, and the client is able to deny the practitioner's inference if it is inaccurate.

In actual use, practitioners paraphrase frequently and reflect feeling and meaning less often. Whereas all these reacting skills contribute to the client experiences of feeling understood, it is reflection of meaning that can create for the client the sense that this person (the practitioner) "really understands what I'm going through, really gets me." However, effective meetings and communication with clients entail using all of the skills in a balanced way and for their intended purposes. Now that we have reviewed the most popular and well-travelled skills—questioning and reacting—let us discuss the skills that are little-known in this field, but extremely powerful for our purposes: structuring skills.

Structuring Skills

Structuring skills function to help clients understand better what is happening in a career development intervention. They can be used to open and close meetings and to add useful, meaningful contextual information along the way. Learners learn more when they have a clear idea of what they are learning and why. Similarly, clients, who can also be thought of as learners, are more engaged in the process and better able to focus on problem-solving if there is a clear sense for them of what they are doing and why. In well-structured meetings, clients have a solid understanding of what they are doing and why it is important to be doing it, what is going to happen, what is happening, and what has happened, along with elements of meaning (e.g., information) relevant to the client's story. For our purposes here, we will limit our discussion of structuring skills to the following three: overviews, summaries, and information giving.

Overviews (OV)

An overview (OV) is a statement at the beginning of a session or part thereof that includes two pieces of information: (1) a plan—what is going to happen, what the practitioner and client are going to do; and (2) a purpose—why it is important. Consider the following example:

> **Practitioner**: Hi John. I'd like to spend the first part of our meeting discussing and asking a few questions about what brings you in today and what concerns you might like support with [plan] and this will help us plan how to proceed and think about the next steps [purpose].

As with all of the intervention-related skills, there are an endless number of ways to exercise these interpersonal skills. What matters for helping interventions is that the skills are used clearly and effectively enough to accomplish their specific function. With overviews, what matters is that the client is left with a clear idea about what is going to happen and why it is important.

Summaries (SU)

Summaries (SU) are a restatement of the main information and themes from an interaction, and as such they would logically be shared at the end of a meeting or at the end of a substantive discussion within the meeting. The purpose of a summary is to organize the content of the meeting or discussion so that the client has a stronger idea about what has been said or accomplished. Much is covered in career development intervention meetings. Clients are not only doing most of the speaking (most of the time, that is), but they are also *thinking* much more than they are *speaking*. Summaries function to tie together or package the content so it can be set aside while other topics are addressed. At their best, summaries are not a listing of content but rather a recounting of key parts, themes, and outcomes. Here is an example:

> **Practitioner**: We've had a chance to discuss the concerns you have about being out of work for the past nine months and how you've been feeling more discouraged in the past month or so. We also discussed your goals to get back into the labour market doing something that would take advantage of your track record as an engineer with Acme for the past 15 years.

Summaries should tie things together without adding additional information; they should summarize what has been said and put it on the shelf, so that the discussion can move to other important things or continue in the next interaction.

Information Giving (IG)

As a skill, information giving (IG) is as it sounds: the provision of information relevant to the client or the client's concerns. Generally, information is born of the career development practitioner's knowledge and/or understanding of a known evidence base. The information has the capacity to help clients (1) expand their understanding of relevant resources, (2) appreciate their own experience differently, or (3) better understand the context in which services are being provided. There are many ways to use information giving. For our purposes in this book, *information giving is the main, and probably the only, skill career development practitioners can use to overtly include mental health awareness and positive mental health outcomes in their practice while working within their boundaries of competence.* Below are three examples of scenarios where information giving supports the role of career development intervention as a contributor to positive mental health. What others can you think of?

1. Providing information about a coping resource relevant to the client's story or concerns:

> **Practitioner**: John, I'm not sure, but here is something that might be of interest. I have a friend who was facing the same financial overwhelm that you are, and she met with a financial counsellor at XYZ services. The service was free, but it led her to make some significant changes in her money and debt management. She also learned to budget, and she has been able to get on top of her financial concerns.

We know what you're thinking—or at least we imagine we do, and we agree. Yes! That is a somewhat long-winded way of telling a client about a free financial counselling service! However, presenting the information about a resource this way makes it contextually relevant (e.g., another person in a similar situation).

2. Using information to validate a client's experience with job loss:

> **Practitioner**: John, you mentioned your experience with depression and anxiety over the past few months since being let go from your position with Acme. One of the things we know for certain—there is a good amount of research to back this up—is that feelings of depression and anxiety are fairly common after people lose a job that they've worked at for a while, especially if only a few people were let go.

In this case, the career development practitioner is referring to the research on job loss and depression and anxiety (see, for example, Brand, 2015). This statement by itself is not an intervention for anxiety, but it does normalize the experience of job loss. Normalizing reduces the demand of John feeling like there is something terribly wrong because he lost his job and is now experiencing symptoms of poor mental health. This information giving validates and normalizes the client experience and reduces demands, thereby reducing stress and, in turn, bolstering positive mental health (as discussed in Chapter 6).

Is it appropriate for career development practitioners to tread into the mental health zone by sharing research results about mental health? We say "yes," because the career development practitioner is sharing a contextually relevant finding about job loss and mental health and is not attempting to intervene directly with the client's mental health concerns. However, it is possible that the above exchange would lead to a more in-depth discussion about the client's experience with depression and anxiety. With this potential direction in mind, consider one more example.

3. Sharing information about the mental health outcomes of career development intervention with a client who has shared mental health concerns:

> **Practitioner**: John, it is really useful to hear what it has been like for you over the past few months. As you mentioned, the stress has been increasing along with the anxiety and depression. Just to be clear and so I'm not working outside my area of expertise, I want us to remember that, of course, I'm a career development practitioner and in my role I'm going to focus primarily on career concerns—on doing what I usually do with the clients I have that have been through similar job loss experiences. This is to help you learn and build the skills that

will equip you to manage your career demands. Another thing we know for certain is that taking this approach, even though we're not focusing on mental health concerns directly, leads to less stress, more hope for the future, and other positive mental health outcomes. The research tells us that engaging in this career development intervention has the potential to boost your mental health and wellbeing. Nonetheless, if you want or need additional support with mental health concerns, I have a list of referral resources I can set you up with.

In this case, the career development practitioner uses information giving to state the limits of their competence, to emphasize that the focus will be on managing career development concerns, and to point out that the evidence suggests a boost in positive mental health may result. This example illustrates an important implication for your practice. We know that mental health resources are scarce, demands are at an all-time high, and services tend to be overwhelmed. As a consequence, having a list of viable referral possibilities is a challenge for most career development practitioners. We think a referral path to mental health practitioners and resources adds greatly to working within the boundaries of your competence. We also think a ready referral path will help to allay much of the fear you might have about discussing mental health evidence with your clients. We provide a structure for developing these resources in Chapter 11.

Of all the skills, we identify information giving as the most powerful for enabling you to both work within your boundaries of competence and for offering a clear way to share mental health evidence with your clients.

Strategies and a Sample Interaction

We now show how practitioner usage of the skills discussed above might create a safe space for clients to talk about mental health in relation to career development, or at minimum, ensure clients leave a session feeling that their mental health concerns have been validated, understood, or normalized. The point here is not to use the skills exactly as illustrated but to be aware that a few shifts in language use can make a big difference in helping clients look at their mental health in relation to their career development.

Before we provide an illustration, it is important to discuss strategy. In a helping context, "strategy" refers to how skills are intentionally combined to bring about particular client outcomes. The basic listening sequence (Ivey, 2003) is a basic strategy for gathering information from a client while letting them know that you understand and validating your understanding. It tends to follow one of two patterns: (1) question – reflection or (2) question – reflection – reflection. Neither asking question after question nor providing reflection after reflection will produce the outcome that the basic listening sequence can produce.

Each skill has its place, and practitioners need to use the skill categories and specific skills intentionally and in the right amounts. Any client meeting will benefit from practitioners doing so as follows:

- Start with an *overview* so the client knows what the practitioner is doing and why it is important.
- Finish with a *summary* so that the client has a clear sense of what happened in the session and what is planned for the future.
- Ask *open questions* and use *declarative probes* to gather information; ask *closed questions* to solicit confirmation.
- *Paraphrase* frequently to check perceptions and let the client know that the practitioner hears the verbal content of what the client is saying.
- *Reflect feeling and meaning* both to communicate inferences about key feelings and important meanings and ultimately to create a sense for the client that they are really understood.
- Use *information giving* to (1) share information about resources, (2) share evidence about career development intervention and positive mental health, or (3) provide information about the practitioner's focus on career development intervention and their limits of competence.

You can plan to do all of the above even if you have no idea what your client wants to talk about. Of course, your plan may change slightly or you may throw it out completely as the interaction unfolds, but this general strategy is necessary and sufficient to bring awareness of, and support for, positive mental health formally into your work as a career development practitioner.

Here is a sample transcript of a practitioner's potential contribution to a client interaction, with the skills identified by their two-letter abbreviations. The language is somewhat formal; in practice you would naturally apply each skill using your own words. To emphasize our main point, this career development practitioner has some general knowledge of mental health and illness, but they are not a mental health practitioner or even a career development practitioner specialized in addressing mental health conditions. Instead, this person is making intentional use of interpersonal skills, especially structuring skills and information giving, to maintain and operate within their boundaries of competence.

> **Practitioner (IG):** We've discussed confidentiality and I'll just mention that I'm a career development practitioner and my main focus will be on the career development concerns you want support with. We know, however, that other parts of our lives are strongly affected by our career-related decisions and activities and vice versa. It's difficult to make effective career decisions without considering our whole life.

> **Practitioner (OV):** For today's meeting, I was thinking we could have a conversation about your career concerns and I may ask some questions and reflect back certain things [plan] so that I can get a better understanding of the type of support you're looking for and so you can have a better understanding as well [purpose].

> **Practitioner (CQ):** Would that be OK with you? [confirmation]

> **Practitioner (OQ):** What would you like to talk about today?

> **Practitioner (PP):** So, a few things there, but the main thing seems to be having lost your job, thinking you would be able to get back to work after a few weeks, but a year later the economy hasn't picked up and there just haven't been opportunities in your previous occupation.

> **Practitioner (OQ):** Generally, how have things been going?

> **Practitioner (RF):** Sounds like it's been getting more stressful and discouraging, especially recently.

Practitioner (IG): One of the things we know for certain about job loss is that it is stressful for most people, that over time it can take its toll on our mental health.

Practitioner (OQ): How has that been for you?

Practitioner (RF): It's been really disappointing, and it's left you feeling pretty inadequate.

Practitioner (OQ): What has been the impact on the other parts of your life?

Practitioner (PP): So, things have carried on at home and with your family, but you've dialed things back in other areas, and haven't been spending time with friends.

Practitioner (OQ): What would you like to see happen?

Practitioner (RM): So, getting back to work, but the most important thing seems to be having cash flow sooner rather than later; that seems to be your priority [inference about values and preferences].

Practitioner (IG): Just to be clear and so I'm not working beyond my competence, I want to let you know that, as I mentioned, I'm a career development practitioner and in my role I'm going to focus primarily on your career concerns, on doing what I usually do with the clients I have that have been through similar job loss experiences. This is to focus on helping you to learn and build the skills that will equip you to manage your career demands. Another thing we know for certain is that taking this approach, even though we're not focusing on mental health concerns directly, leads to less stress, more hope for the future, and other positive mental health outcomes. The research tells us that engaging in this career development intervention has the potential to boost your mental health. However, if you want or need additional support with mental health concerns, I have a list of referral resources and I would be happy to help you connect with one of them if that would be of interest to you.

Practitioner (SU): Just tying things together here, you haven't been able to find work in your area for the past year, it's been very stressful personally, and it's impacted some other important parts of your life [restatement of the main information and themes from the meeting].

The practitioner in the above example uses the full range of skills we have outlined in this chapter. There are many other skills we have not covered, but the skills we have included here are, we think, the most important for our purposes vis-à-vis mental health outcomes. Used intentionally, with practice, and with feedback from clients, they make it possible to include mental health awareness and positive mental health outcomes in your career development practice. Of course, on the front lines of career development intervention, nobody actually talks like the practitioner in our sample transcript. To apply the skills and strategies yourself, in your own words and context, remember their functions and use them accordingly. The possibilities are endless.

Summary

In this chapter we reviewed generic interpersonal skills that can be used effectively to include mental health awareness and positive mental health support in your role as a career development practitioner. Basic questioning and reacting skills were reviewed. We paid particular attention to the category of structuring skills and the specific skill of information giving. Information giving is likely the skill most relevant to including mental health awareness in your career development practice.

Reflection Questions

1. We are confident you have used all of the interpersonal skills discussed in this chapter in some form with your clients, whether you know it or not. In your work with clients to date, to what extent have you intentionally used specific skills to bring about client outcomes?

2. Of the skills discussed in this chapter, which ones, if practised and mastered, would most benefit your work with clients?

3. How might you go about further developing your ability to intentionally use these skills in your day-to-day work?

Evaluating is itself the most valuable treasure of all that we value. It is only through evaluation that value exists: and without evaluation the nut of existence would be hollow.

Frederic Nietzsche

To Ponder...

Think of a group of clients or students who experienced mental health benefits from the work you did with them. How did you know these benefits were accrued? How were the benefits documented?

10. Tracking Mental Health Outcomes in Career Development Practice

Imagine this: It's launch day for the new website of your employment services organization. You have contributed content to the site but today is the first time you see it in its finished form. You open the site in your browser and see that not only does it beautifully describe your team's talents and services, it has a rotating banner that highlights key results of your organization's services. Along with the basics, such as client satisfaction levels and employment outcomes, the banner cycles through a raft of other information about your last year's outcomes:

- 80% of employed clients obtained work they described as "good work."
- 70% of employed clients obtained "good work" that fit with their talents and aspirations.
- Clients improved their career management competencies by 60%.
- Clients' coping abilities increased by 40% by end-of-program; 70% one year after.

- 90% of clients' feelings of hope—a key mental health outcome—increased by more than 50%.
- 82% of clients reported "substantial" improvements in self-efficacy—a key mental health and employability outcome.
- 95% of employed clients' levels of social acceptance—a key mental health outcome—improved "to a great extent" as measured six months after the program.
- 96% of clients who did not become employed report "significantly improved" ability to manage their lives.
- Clients averaged a 30% increase in World Health Organization Well-Being Index scores.

Then you notice something else at the bottom of the screen, in an acknowledgements section listing the names and logos of key contributors: Two organizations devoted to mental health are co-funders of some of your programming!

After you have wiped the tears of joy from your eyes (surely we are not the only ones to get emotional about such results), you reflect on how little extra effort it took to obtain this outcome information—information that shows the broad impact of your work to future clients, funders, collaborating organizations, and policy-makers, and that was likely vital to obtaining funding from mental health organizations.

Evaluating the mental health impacts of career development intervention need not be complicated or difficult for you or your clients. The results of evaluations, however, can exert enormous influence over funding, resource allocations, client buy-in, improved practice, and your own feeling of making a difference. A little effort toward evaluation can often yield large returns for your practice.

We cannot and do not address all the nuances of evaluation in this chapter, of course. Here we provide information regarding some key evaluation ideas pertinent to career development—mental health connections:

- The meaning of "evidence-based" in the context of career development and mental health
- Evaluation as an education/awareness and improvement activity
- Evaluation as a negotiated activity
- Practical measures to gather meaningful evidence

We believe these ideas will put you on the path to incorporating mental health outcomes in your evaluations.

We assume that you are interested in obtaining the explicit endorsement of funders or other stakeholders before you proceed with evaluating mental health outcomes, but you may not be. If this is the case, you can skip directly to the section titled "Sample Evaluation Questions." Before you do, however, we invite you to consider the potential value of having the support, involvement, and endorsement of key stakeholders such as funders and the leadership within your organization as you evaluate mental health outcomes. Involved and supportive stakeholders may

- bring ideas to the evaluation that you had not thought of;
- provide resources, such as funds, to support evaluation processes;
- allow you the time you need to address evaluation requirements;
- be far more receptive to and interested in positive findings produced by the evaluation; and/or
- be more likely to help rather than criticize in the event that evaluation efforts do not initially provide positive results (i.e., if the results are not as favourable as expected, an involved stakeholder may help troubleshoot problems and solutions with you rather than dismissing the entire idea).

Having said all this, we recognize that it may be easier to communicate the value of evaluating mental health outcomes to select stakeholders *after* you have collected some data showing the mental health impact of your work.

What Qualifies as Evidence

You have likely heard the term "evidence-based" bandied about by funders and administrators. In general, it refers to making decisions about services and practices on the basis of reasonable research evaluation involving objective data,[11] collected by you or others, about

---

[11] Objective data can include subjective responses to programs and services. Client satisfaction surveys, for example, capture clients' subjective perspectives in a way that is objective and therefore verifiable.

the services and practices. The expectation that services, programs, and products should be based on evidence is a reasonable one. Some funders may be interested in untested, experimental approaches that are well conceived, but few, if any, funders want to devote resources to something that is entirely speculative.

"Evidence-based" is not the same as "proven." It is very difficult to prove the effectiveness of human services. Most funders, policy-makers, and administrators recognize the distinction between proof and evidence, and most will not demand proof.[12] Whether something constitutes "evidence" or not is largely up to the beholder. For some, client testimonials of success may be considered evidence, but not sufficient evidence on which to make decisions. For others, data regarding objective outcomes (e.g., employment, test achievement) are required. Most stakeholders want more than testimonials but accept testimonials as part of a package of evidence. The important point here is that what qualifies as evidence for one funder or stakeholder may not do so for another. Evidence is something that is agreed upon by the various players; there is no independent standard. As such, evidence is something to be discussed and negotiated. Discussions, negotiations, and agreements all require parties to educate and understand each other, an activity we turn to next.

Understanding Stakeholder Interests and Motivations

It is prudent to check what each relevant stakeholder believes "evidence-based" means and what domains of evidence are important to them. Before you can make a case for evidence sources, recognize that funders and administrators can have very different perspectives on career development work than you do.

---

[12] We hope you appreciate irony, because we have no substantive evidence that this claim is true! We do, however, have a great deal of experience working with governments and agencies (federal, provincial, and municipal), First Nations' administrations, private-sector organizations, and chari-table organizations over the last 30 years, none of which have ever demanded proof.

Let's take a government funder as an example. The government representative who actually works with your organization and administers the funds on behalf of the government may never have met an unemployed client, provided career development services to clients, taken training in career development or employment services, or have an interest in career development. They may be keenly interested in working in government because of the security and benefits government work can offer, and because of the opportunities for career advancement: to work their way up in a government department, transfer to another department (say, transportation), and become a senior administrator of a branch of government. The department they end up in may be incidental; their level in the organizational structure may be the important element of their goals. This person, who may be managing their career path decisions exceptionally well, may appear by their actions and attitude toward your organization to be uncaring, bureaucratic, and inflexible.

To get this hypothetical government representative to pay attention to the things you want, such as mental health outcomes, you really need to understand their aims and their interests or motives. Ask yourself, "How will measuring mental health outcomes help them reach their goals?" Of course, you could ask the person directly, but you will likely be met with a blank stare and the answer "Measuring mental health outcomes won't help me." This is where building awareness and readiness come in. This person will almost certainly not have devoted any time or energy to thinking about mental health outcomes. Obtaining their support for and interest in mental health outcomes begins with letting them know of the connections between your services and mental health outcomes. Only after they have a sense of this can you broach the discussion of how evaluating mental health outcomes may be in their best interests.

What might those interests be? A better understanding of the broader impact of career development work may enable your government funder to

- make more effective arguments to their management about the return on investment of funds going to your services and services like yours;
- make better decisions and more effectively defend these decisions when short-term versus long-term choices need to be made (e.g., funding many low-quality programs with decent

short-term results or funding fewer high-quality programs that obtain both short-term results and long-term gains);

- show their management they are proactively seeking to add value, and thereby using public funds effectively;

- show their management they are actively supporting improvements in programs and services; and/or

- put their management on a better footing to work horizontally with other units within the department or with other government departments.

This list of possible stakeholder interests and motivations applies equally to private funders, foundation funders, and internal funders (e.g., a career centre within a corporation relies on internal funding decisions typically made by senior leadership). For non-government funders, the need to work horizontally may be with other departments within their organization, or with external organizations.

You will not know your stakeholders' interests until you or someone in your organization develops a relationship with them. As you get to know them, you can begin thinking about how to frame your one-to-one "awareness campaign" regarding the mental health outcomes of career development intervention, and why it is important to measure this impact.

Negotiating and Collaborating

We mentioned above that the domains and criteria for evidence-gathering are negotiated, not set in stone. Your organization, as well as funders of your programs and services, almost certainly have a few "must-have" variables (e.g., client satisfaction, employment, student grades) to be measured. All other evaluation is open to discussion and negotiation after these are taken care of. As you work to develop stakeholders' awareness of career development and mental health connections and to understand stakeholders' motivations and interests, you can collaborate with them to choose variables to measure, ways to measure them, and what to do with the findings, all bearing in mind ethical constraints regarding evaluation.

Be clear about your own motives and discuss them with stakeholders. These may include:

- improving your practice to be more intentional (and successful) regarding mental health outcomes,
- advocating for your practice through the use of evidence showing that career development intervention does far more than simply get people employed,
- improving the field of career development by helping establish an evidence base regarding career development and positive mental health,
- connecting your practice more effectively to related practices and interventions (e.g., mental health interventions) by clearly identifying what your practice can assist clients with and what it cannot assist with, and
- advocating for the funding and/or creation of more resources for your client group (e.g., using data to illustrate shortfalls in mental health services and other services—shortfalls that prevent your clients from succeeding).

Ponder these motives as you read the next sections about measuring mental health outcomes and selecting outcomes worth measuring.

Selecting Indicators of Mental Health to Measure

If you are interested in measuring the mental health outcomes of your practice but not very interested in why we make the measurement recommendations that we make, you can skip ahead to "Sample Evaluation Questions." Otherwise, allow us to walk you through our thinking about how to determine what to measure so as to reveal mental health changes effectively in practical, real-world situations (e.g., an employment service in which clients may tolerate only three more questions before they become completely exasperated with completing a survey!). We do so because there are many directions to go in this regard. By understanding our reasoning you may better be able to choose and justify a different way of going on this.

Rationale

Measuring changes in mental health is made difficult by the absence of a universal definition of mental health. As we have noted elsewhere in this book, some definitions have happiness as an indicator, or component, whereas others do not. Some include personal growth; others do not. Some use different terms for what might be the same indicator. How different is "happiness" from "positive affect," for example? Are "meaning" and "purpose" different? Is "accomplishment" a by-product of "environmental mastery" or are these distinct concepts?

The definitional problem becomes a little more complicated when one looks at the core concept of an "indicator" and the way it is measured. For example, the most popular measure of mental health is the WHO (Five) Well-Being Index, a five-item measure developed by the World Health Organization (Figure 10.1). "Calm and relaxed" is one of the five indicators, yet there is no definition of mental health that includes the concepts "calm" or "relaxed." These are clearly pointers to a broader indicator, the ability to cope. Coping skills or the perceptions of coping ability are common to several definitions of mental health.

Psychiatric Research Unit
WHO Collaborating Centre in Mental Health

WHO (Five) Well-Being Index (1998 version)

Please indicate for each of the five statements which is closest to how you have been feeling over the last two weeks. Notice that higher numbers mean better well-being.

Example: If you have felt cheerful and in good spirits more than half of the time during the last two weeks, put a tick in the box with the number 3 in the upper right corner.

	Over the last two weeks	All of the time	Most of the time	More than half of the time	Less than half of the time	Some of the time	At no time
1	**I have felt cheerful and in good spirits**	5	4	3	2	1	0
2	**I have felt calm and relaxed**	5	4	3	2	1	0
3	**I have felt active and vigorous**	5	4	3	2	1	0
4	**I woke up feeling fresh and rested**	5	4	3	2	1	0
5	**My daily life has been filled with things that interest me**	5	4	3	2	1	0

Figure 10.1. **WHO (Five) Well-Being Index (1998 Version).** From https://www.psykiatri-regionh.dk/who-5/who-5-questionnaires/Pages/default.aspx

If career development practitioners are to measure changes in mental health, it is important that the indicators they measure are, ideally:

- significantly related to mental health, so that the measures are pointing to the right thing;
- understood by stakeholders (e.g., funders, policy-makers, clients) as related to mental health, so that there can be buy-in to the career development–mental health connection;

- relevant to practice (i.e., the changes they are examining are ones they would expect to see), so that practitioners are motivated to implement the measurement process;
- sensitive to changes that can reasonably be expected even with modest interventions, so that the changes can be discerned;
- relevant to clients' perceptions of the service, so that the measures do not seem intrusive; and
- credible to the academic/research community, so that practitioners' measures are not dismissed or critiqued as irrelevant or 'fluff.'

For example, consider one indicator: feelings of hope. Working backwards through the above list, we see that hope is

- the focus of a great deal of research,
- relevant to clients' perceptions of the service,
- a variable with discernable changes with even brief interventions,
- extremely relevant to the practice of career development (i.e., it is a sign for practitioners that the interventions are moving in the right direction),
- generally understood by all stakeholders, albeit in slightly different ways, *but* as described in Chapter 5, *not* part of any dominant definition of mental health!

Just because hope is not explicitly identified as a component of mental health in any definition does not mean we abandon its measurement, particularly since it fulfils every other criterion in the list. It simply means we need to connect hope with an indicator that *is* part of a definition. Recall from Chapter 5 that the most common definition of hope in the research literature is "the perceived capability to derive pathways to desired goals, and motivate oneself via agency thinking to use those pathways" (Snyder, 2002, p. 249). This means that hope exists when the individual assesses themselves capable of

- figuring out what needs to be done to reach their goals (pathways thinking), and
- doing the things that need to be done to reach their goals (agency thinking).

Hope is thus easily tied to at least one very common component of definitions of mental health: coping. "Agency thinking" is the perception of being able to cope, to deal with the challenges that one will face. "Pathways thinking" can also be seen as part of coping; this kind of thinking predicts what is needed and anticipates the demands that will accompany these needs. Coping strategies involve pacing one's progress to ensure the demands remain manageable.

This covers our rationale for selecting indicators of mental health to serve a variety of purposes. Next, we review the actual indicators we recommend using. Bear in mind, however, that gathering evidence for changes in mental health is a negotiated process between you, your administration, and your funder. These other parties may have different ideas about the evidence they would like to gather than we do.

Recommendations

The eight indicators of mental health that we recommend measuring are shared by three or more of 12 currently accepted definitions of mental health from a range of academic and public health perspectives. Given our aim to ensure relevance to and buy-in from various stakeholders, researchers, and, of course, practitioners, we found seven substantive definitions of mental health in the psychological literature, one operational definition in the health world, and definitions used by Australia, Canada, the United States, and the World Health Organization. Some of these definitions are intended for public consumption and policy-making and others are intended for theory-building and/or research (e.g., Keyes's dual continua model). Each definition lays out components—indicators or signs—of mental health. The most common indicators among these definitions are as follows (the number in parentheses indicates the number of definitions that include the indicator):

- Meaning/purpose (5)
- Environmental mastery (5)
- Coping skills (4)
- Autonomy (4)
- Relationships (4)
- Contribution (4)

- Positive affect/happiness (4)
- Self-acceptance (3)

Each of these indicators can be measured via self-report reasonably easily (see sample questions and surveys below).

You may be wondering why we did not simply choose one theoretical model of mental health and use the indicators related to that model. We certainly considered this, but the main problem is that there does not seem to be a universally accepted theoretical model. Each has its "fan base" (and probably deservedly so) that would be unable to fully accept the use of another model. We might pick a model and advocate for it if our aim was to change how everyone thinks about mental health. Our aim, however, is to have as many stakeholders as possible see how career development contributes to their understanding of desirable mental health outcomes. We have hedged our bets by looking to commonalities.

Lucky for us, Corey Keyes also hedged his bets (although we are not sure he would phrase it this way), borrowing emotional wellbeing indicators from researchers such as Seligman (1990), psychological wellbeing indicators from Ryff (1989), and social wellbeing indicators from a variety of sociologists (Westerhof & Keyes, 2010). Even more fortunately for us, Keyes's dual continua model seems to be gaining an increasing amount of support in different health-related communities. The Public Health Agency of Canada's Centre for Chronic Disease Prevention, for example, use Keyes's indicators of mental health (as well as some additional indicators, many of which are related to environmental factors such as workplace environment or levels of community violence) in its Positive Mental Health Surveillance Indicator Framework (Centre for Chronic Disease Prevention, 2016). The framework, which draws upon a number of data sources, is what the agency uses to monitor community mental health.

In this section, we provide sample questions to use in verbal interactions with clients as well as questions to add to existing client surveys. We include also a short survey regarding mental health outcomes specifically for your use or adaptation.

A word of caution: We noted earlier that evaluation items need to be relevant to clients' perceptions of the service being evaluated. For example, it would likely seem jarring to participants in a three-hour job-search-documentation workshop if you asked them to rate the workshop's impact on the quality of their marriage or romantic relationships. They would likely not see a connection and they would find such a question nosey, intrusive, and irrelevant. A question after such a workshop on "mental health improvement" or "mental illness difficulties" would seem only slightly less intrusive. (A brief critique of graduate wellbeing questions by Johnson [2019] illustrates this point.) However, questions about coping, hope, and anxiety, especially when connected to the world of work, would likely make sense to most clients.

Verbal Questions

The great advantage to asking clients to report on how they have changed is the sheer richness of the information you get back. You will hear stories, examples, details, and depth that you cannot get in a typical written survey. The disadvantage is that you can get a great deal of information that is hard to make sense of overall and therefore to report on when compared to a numerical survey.

If you are inclined to ask evaluative questions of your clients regarding their experiences and changes, consider the following questions related to mental health outcomes:

- How has your thinking changed about handling the demands coming up in your life since you started [the workshop, course, counselling...]?

- How have your feelings changed about handling the demands coming up in your life since you started [the workshop, course, counselling...]?

- How have your behaviours or actions changed related to handling the demands coming up in your life since you started [the workshop, course, counselling...]?

These three open questions about cognition, affect, and behaviour can capture a great deal of information. Add the following question if you want more-specific information regarding your interventions and the client's answers to any/all of these questions:

- What, specifically, caused this change?

This question will help you determine if your intervention was the cause (compared to some other event in the client's life) and, if so, perhaps which component of the intervention really made a difference.

Written Questions

The following questions pertaining to mental health could be added to existing surveys you provide to clients (all can be answered with a Likert-type scale going from 0 to 5 or 0 to 10, where 0 is "not at all" and 5 or 10 is "completely," depending on your or your agency's preference):

- How hopeful are you about finding work?
- How hopeful are you about your ability to manage your future career path?
- How competent do you feel regarding [insert a skill set of interest, e.g., resumé-writing, interviewing, cold-calling]?
- How competent do you feel regarding your ability to manage your future career path?
- How positive is your thinking about your ability to handle the demands coming up in your life?
- How calm are you about the demands coming up in your life?
- How well do your actions directly address the demands that you face in life?

Do not get hung up on the specific phrasing. For example, the last three questions above could easily be adapted for a scale with "completely disagree" at one end and "completely agree" at another:

- I think positively about my ability to handle the demands coming up in my life.
- I feel calm about the demands that are coming up in my life.
- I act in ways that directly address the demands I face in life.

Sample Surveys

One way of asking clients about change is to have them indicate how they felt about an attribute or characteristic before and after an intervention. This can be done by having clients complete two surveys, a pre-intervention survey and then a post-intervention survey, or it can be done in a post-intervention survey that asks about both "post" and "pre." The details of the rationale for this retrospective Post-Pre Assessment can be found in Hiebert and Magnusson's (2014) description of evaluation in career development practice. For the current purposes, consider four main advantages to the "post-pre" approach rather than the traditional pre-test/post-test approach in day-to-day practice:

- It is easier because only one survey is distributed.

- It is easier to see individual change as well as group change—and we mean "see" literally: The client's before and after responses are on one page!

- Post-Pre Assessment is as easily completed after brief interventions (e.g., a one-hour, one-to-one session) as it is after long, involved interventions (e.g., a 10-week program involving numerous components).

- Clients may be able to answer more effectively because they know more about what you are asking *after* the intervention. In true pre-post surveys, there is a risk of asking clients to rate something for which they just do not know enough. For example, the average person thinks they know how to write a resumé and typically rates themself as average or better. However, once they have taken a resumé-writing workshop, they realize all the things that they did not know. A pre-post test in this scenario can often result in clients showing that they are *less* competent at writing resumés at the end of the workshop than they were before the workshop! However, if provided with a "post-pre" survey *after* the workshop, clients are likely to indicate how much more they know.

The sample four-item survey in Figure 10.2 uses the Post-Pre Assessment method to solicit clients' thoughts, feelings, and behaviours related to mental health. The longer survey in Figure 10.3 asks about all eight indicators of mental health that we recommend tracking (referred to earlier in this chapter). Either could be used after an intervention such as a workshop or program.

Instructions: Use the following scale to rate your "before" and "after" experience related to [today's workshop, our counselling sessions, the employability program, etc.].

Unacceptable		Acceptable		
0	1	2	3	4

I was / I am...	Before	After
1. Feeling hopeful about my future.		
2. Thinking positively about my ability to handle the demands coming up in my life.		
3. Feeling calm about the demands coming up in my life.		
4. Acting in ways to directly address the demands I'm facing in my life.		

Figure 10.2. **Sample post-pre assessment survey.**

Use the following scale to rate your "before" and "after" experience related to today's workshop.

Unacceptable		Acceptable		
0	1	2	3	4

	Before	After
1. I have a sense of purpose and/or meaning about my life and career path.		
2. In general, I am able to manage my demands and activities in a way that meets my needs; I feel I am in charge of my life.		
3. I am confident I will be able cope with the most important demands I am facing.		
4. In important parts of my life, I am able to make decisions that align with my own values, interests, and preferences.		
5. I have positive, supportive relationships with others.		
6. I believe my activities are useful and valued by society and others.		
7. I feel positive about life.		
8. I feel positive about myself.		

Figure 10.3. **Sample post-pre assessment survey for common mental health indicators.**

Michael designed and regularly facilitates a three-hour career exploration workshop at Mount Royal University in Calgary, Alberta, Canada. A number of career-related issues are addressed, including self-awareness, world of work exploration, and decision-making strategies. At no point are either "hope" or "optimism" addressed in the workshop. With this in mind, see Figure 10.4 for sample results from the Post-Pre Assessment Michael distributes at the end of the workshop.

Unacceptable		Acceptable		
0	1	2	3	4

	Before	After	Difference
1. Understanding the role of interests in making better career decisions.	1.78	3.46	1.68
2. Understanding the role of values in making better career decisions.	1.83	3.33	1.5
3. Understanding the role of strengths and best skills in making better career decisions.	2.20	3.37	1.17
4. Understanding how to plan for combining work with other life roles.	1.63	3.25	1.62
5. Understanding of my needs and criteria for a future career path and how to use for future career decisions.	1.89	3.35	1.46
6. Understanding how to research career options (educational and occupational possibilities).	1.84	3.75	1.9
7. Understanding how to better cope with barriers and obstacles that could prevent me from pursuing desired career paths.	1.63	3.14	1.51
8. Hope and optimism about finding work I enjoy after graduation.	1.75	3.57	1.82*
9. Hope and optimism about finding meaningful work in areas I hadn't been considering.	1.69	3.03	1.33
10. Knowledge and understanding of my future goals related to career planning.	1.89	3.19	1.30

Second highest difference score is on a mental health outcome not addressed in the workshop!

Figure 10.4. Post-pre assessment survey for career exploration workshop.

The highest difference score, indicating the greatest change between "before" and "after," is "understanding how to research career options," which makes perfect sense given the workshop's title. The second highest difference score is "hope and optimism about finding work I enjoy after graduation," even though this is not a topic addressed in the workshop! Notice the size of the difference, too: On a 5-point scale, students rate their hope and optimism as "unacceptable" (just under 2) before, but as closer to "completely acceptable" (4) than "acceptable" (3) after. If these were percentages, Michael would report 44% hope and optimism acceptability levels before and 89% acceptability levels after! This is quite remarkable in a three-hour intervention.

Over time, it is our hope that the career development community agrees on the key mental health outcomes to measure and, perhaps, on how to measure these outcomes as well. If so, career development practitioners in schools, employment offices, post-secondary institutions, agencies, and private companies could better compare mental health outcomes across settings as well as the interventions that led to those outcomes. The importance of this will become clear in the next chapter, which deals with influencing those who have influence, such as funders and policy-makers.

Summary

Gathering evidence of career development intervention's impact on mental health is essential if the field is to make the case that this impact exists. Evidence, which is different from proof, need not be difficult to obtain. Discussions with relevant stakeholders can lead to agreements about what reasonably constitutes evidence so that collected data are meaningful to all concerned. There are numerous components to mental health (e.g., purpose, environmental mastery, autonomy) and a variety of ways to measure these components (e.g., verbal questions, written surveys). You need not measure each component in every way; the key to making evidence-gathering manageable is agreement among key stakeholders regarding the minimum that will suffice.

Reflection Questions

1. What are your own personal indicators of mental health? How do you track them?

2. What indicators could you easily use to track mental health changes experienced by your clients or students?

3. What is one area of measurement or evaluation you would be well-served to learn more about? How could you engage in this learning?

All social change starts with a conversation.

Margaret J. Wheatley

To Ponder...

Consider a time when, whether by luck or planning, an important decision-maker implemented a program or service you were hoping for. Remember how that felt!

11. Engaging Allies and Stakeholders: From the Inside Out

We began this book by describing the need to have others (e.g., typical stakeholders as well as the general public) see the mental health value of career development services. We worry that, in some settings, these services may be displaced by symptom-focused mental health efforts. We want and need to help stakeholders of all kinds see the mental health impact of career development. We suspect you feel this need as well. Think about how great it would be if your organization's administration, funders, clients (which may include students and their parents), as well as allied professionals in mental health, social work, and medicine, were aware of the mental health impact of your work and valued your services for both the direct and indirect outcomes they achieve.

Wouldn't it be convenient if merely providing information could change people's minds and motives? It would be easy to send stakeholders pamphlets outlining the various mental health outcomes to which career development services contribute if doing so meant everyone would then see and support the broader benefits of your work. As any government election has revealed, however, information is only a small, albeit important, part of the influencing process.

It is well beyond the scope of this book—and likely beyond the scope of your role—to fully address all of the efforts needed to engage relevant stakeholders in the idea of connecting career development activities to mental health outcomes. We will focus on the need for communication and advocacy, but we do so with the full understanding that you are a career development practitioner who already has a job serving clients and who is not looking for another job, the job of changing people's hearts and minds. However, we also recognize that the job you have exists because someone knows that your role fills an important need. Just as self-promotion is increasingly a requirement of effective career development (and something you probably discuss with your clients), so is role-promotion a requirement if the career development field is to thrive. With this in mind, we lay out a strategic approach to awareness-building that will enable you to act effectively without feeling the need to either become a marketing expert or divert energy away from client service. This approach moves from the inside—your head and heart—to as far outside—colleagues, clients, managers, funders—as your motivation and capacity permit. In this chapter, we move away from theoretical justifications and evidence bases and provide instead step-by-step instruction. We do so under the assumption that engagement may not be something you want to understand deeply but something you want to do reasonably efficiently.

The method we describe is based on "inside-out marketing," an approach we learned from our mentor, colleague, and Canadian career development guru, Barrie Day. A relentless innovator in the career development field, Barrie recognized that the complexity of career development intervention required a marketing approach quite different from what one would use to generate interest for a product such as a household cleaner or motorcycle. With mass-produced products, it is fine to market by way of exposure via billboards, web advertisements, and radio spots. This "outside-in" approach is all about increasing sales and market share by getting attention and creating name recognition. Outside-in approaches are problematic with products and services that are intended to actually change the person and their motivation by increasing understanding, awareness, and skill. There are a few reasons for this, the most important of which are that outside-in approaches cannot account for individual uniqueness in undergoing change and cannot help a person carry through a change process.[13] The marketing, influencing, and persuading work needed involves something different than just getting someone to buy a product; it requires "buyers," in your case stakeholders, to embark on a change process—to see and engage with services and the outcomes of those services differently. Hence, inside-out marketing is really an approach to creating engagement.

Creating change in motivation and behaviour requires trusting relationships and time. You would not say to a client "All the research shows that you'll be better off when you stop complaining and get a job" with the expectation of positive behaviour change. Similarly, saying to a funder "All the research shows that career development intervention leads to positive mental health outcomes so you should keep funding me" is unlikely to change their behaviour. Inside-out engagement works gradually. It begins with the marketer's head (ideas, knowledge) and heart (values, conviction), works outward via trusted relationships with allies and stakeholders, and is continually adjusted as feedback is received (Figure 11.1).

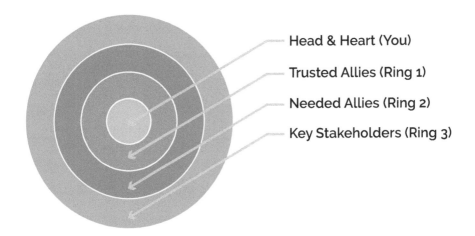

Figure 11.1. **Inside-out marketing.**

---

[13] You may have encountered Prochaska and DiClemente's (1983) transtheoretical model of change in which change begins with the movement from pre-contemplation (no thoughts of change) to contemplation (thinking that change might be a good thing) and then on through preparation (making plans to change), action (making the change), and maintenance (sticking with the change). Mass marketing may be helpful in moving people from pre-contemplation to contemplation. It will not, however, help people with further movement.

In the "how-to" sections that follow, we focus on creating engagement with those in your own organization, and we prompt you to identify your values, messages, and allies. Later in the chapter, we examine engagement among allied professionals, particularly mental health professionals. If there are others in your practice/organization who are also keenly interested in communicating the mental health outcomes of your practice/services, we invite you to collaborate—treat your group as one "head and heart" and answer the questions in this chapter together.

Steps to Inside-Out Engagement

Clarify Your Head and Heart

The starting point for your inside-out marketing effort is clarifying your own head and heart. With regard to your "head," this means clearly establishing in your own mind what you know about career development and mental health in general (i.e., the evidence base) and in your own practice (which you will continuously be getting information about if you have initiated your own evaluation system, as per Chapter 10).

When thinking about your head, consider the knowledge you have that is most rock-solid for you, even if it is based on a combination of others' research and your own experience rather than on data from your own practice. For example, in Chapter 4 we reviewed career development interventions that increase hope or build capacity. Your practice may be particularly effective at one of these types of interventions, and you may have a wealth of anecdotal evidence regarding their mental health outcomes. For example, if you help clients with resumés or interview skills, you might be aware of changes in hope, confidence, stress, or self-esteem. This is the sort of skill/knowledge area to clarify for yourself prior to undertaking any marketing efforts.

As a partial aside, if you were garnering support for a new intervention or program, or an embellishment to an existing intervention or program, part of clarifying head would be articulating the nature of the program or embellishment so that you would have a firm base on which to build your marketing efforts. If incorporating evaluation of mental health outcomes is an embellishment you are considering, clarifying head would involve ensuring you are completely comfortable with the approach you would take (as discussed in the previous chapter).

Head

What can you confidently identify as the top three mental health outcomes from your work as a career development practitioner, and what are the specific practices or interventions that contribute to those outcomes?

"Heart" refers to the values, beliefs, convictions, and interests that propel you to want others to be aware of and endorse career development intervention as mental health intervention. You may think that everyone in the career development field shares the same heart in this regard, but consider all of the following possible motives/values, which may or may not be driving your efforts:

- Security (e.g., "I don't want my funding cut because I'll lose my income")
- Efficiency (e.g., "My work not only helps people become employed, it may save mental health and mental illness-related costs, too")
- Effectiveness (e.g., "My work starts at the root of potential mental health concerns; effort at my end saves grief and more effort later on")
- Self-Sufficiency (e.g., "My work helps my clients look after themselves more effectively and this means their whole selves, which includes mental health")
- Growth (e.g., "My work helps clients/students develop capacity, capacity that will help them deal with many of life's demands")
- Recognition (e.g., "Why can't people see that we do so much more than just help people get employed?")

None of these values is "right" or "wrong," "good" or "bad"; they simply are what they are. Clarifying heart is not about judging your values but clearly laying them out on the table for yourself. "Faking it," or trying to show you care about things you do not really care about, will almost inevitably backfire by causing you to lose your motivation, creating distrust with stakeholders, or creating confusion and misunderstanding through mixed messages.

> ## Heart
>
> Reflect on what you most care about (your values) that compels you to get the message out about career development and mental health. What are your top three values?

Identify Stakeholders

Ring 1: Trusted Allies

In Figure 11.1, concentric rings surround Head & Heart (You). Your next job is to identify the stakeholders in each ring. The first ring, Trusted Allies, should be populated by highly trusted individuals, typically colleagues and close friends. The objective here is to begin spreading your message to people you trust and who trust you enough that they will

- listen fully to your idea with an open mind, trusting your good intentions;
- ask questions as they listen so that they have greater clarity, also *forcing you to further clarify your head and heart*;
- provide feedback about your ideas (not about you) and how they may or may not work, *forcing you to further clarify your head and heart*;
- anticipate other stakeholders' reactions and help you overcome possible objections, *forcing you to further clarify your head and heart*;
- help you connect with colleagues and stakeholders they trust (and who trust them) in Ring 2, Needed Allies; and

- share your head and heart with colleagues and stakeholders they trust (and who trust them) in Ring 2, Needed Allies.

As you can see from our repetition of the phrase "forcing you to further clarify your head and heart," a primary aim of connecting with trusted allies is to strengthen both your conviction (heart) and ideas (head). This strengthening will occur because of the trust between you and these trusted colleagues/stakeholders. If you move prematurely to communicate with people with whom mutual trust may be weak, the risks are high for misunderstandings and judgement on their part, followed by defensiveness and inner uncertainty on your part. Remember that ideas/ practices that require people to change typically need to "bring people along" slowly. Early rejection because you moved too quickly will not help your cause and may prejudice others' thinking later.

Trusted Allies

Think of individuals whom you trust and who you believe trust you. Which of these individuals would possibly have an interest in promoting career development intervention as mental health intervention, and may be able to garner support with needed allies? Can you think of up to five trusted allies? You may want to revisit this list after identifying the remaining stakeholders.

Ring 2: Needed Allies

As you and your trusted allies go back and forth with your idea, helping you clarify your head and heart and hone your message, your trusted allies will begin to suggest people they know who would either endorse your idea or have useful feedback to contribute. These people, with whom your trusted allies have trusting relationships even if you do not, will form part of the population of Ring 2, Needed Allies.

Another group of needed allies are individuals who have strong relationships with both your trusted allies (Ring 1) and key stakeholders (Ring 3). In other words, individuals in Ring 2 ideally are the connectors between those you really trust and the key stakeholders you would like to influence.

Consider, for example, a career educator in a high school whose trusted allies (Ring 1) are a social studies teacher, a work experience coordinator, and a physical education teacher. The career educator would like to be more explicit about career development and mental health outcomes in the classroom and actively promote career development education's mental health outcomes to students, potential students, and their parents. The career educator is passionate about individual self-determination—that students should make their choices with the full awareness of the impact of those choices. Being explicit about the full implications of career development for wellbeing would serve this passion well. Doing so, however, would require the endorsement of the principal and at least one vice-principal. Support from the parent council would also be helpful.

The career educator is reasonably new to the school and does not know the principal or vice-principals well, nor do they know anyone on the parent council. The social studies teacher in Ring 1, however, is a close colleague of the social studies team lead, who has worked extensively with the principal over the years. The career educator has this team lead's name in Ring 2 as a needed ally. The work experience coordinator has worked with the parent council over the years and currently knows one particular parent on council very well. This parent's name is in Ring 2 (Needed Allies) and Ring 3 (Key Stakeholders) as a result. The physical education teacher has been at the school for a very long time, is well-respected, and knows everyone. The physical education teacher offers to talk with an influential, academically focused math teacher who is highly suspicious of any career development activity in the school. The physical education teacher knows that this math teacher can tarnish an idea quickly and widely and needs to be brought on board sooner rather than later. The math teacher is also very well-respected, and both school administrators and parent council members will pay serious attention to the two teachers' views. The career educator places the math teacher's name in Ring 2 as a needed ally.

We will come back to this scenario after describing Ring 3, Key Stakeholders, below.

Needed Allies

Think of up to five individuals who could potentially be influential in garnering support from decision-makers. As you do so, recognize that there will likely be needed allies you do not yet know about yet. These will be identified by those in your first ring of trusted allies.

Ring 3: Key Stakeholders

Key stakeholders are the ultimate targets for inside-out marketing and awareness-building. These are the individuals whose endorsement of a concept is needed to

- initiate new practices/methods,
- change policy and procedures,
- advocate with a wider range of stakeholders, and
- allocate resources in different ways.

In the career educator's case described above, the key stakeholders are the school's administrators (with the most important being the school principal) and the parent council members. These individuals were easily identified by the career educator. However, as the career educator engaged in discussions with trusted allies and needed allies, it became very apparent that one of the school's guidance counsellors was a key stakeholder because both the school administration and parent council took that person's advice on these matters almost as gospel. The career educator therefore added the guidance counsellor to Ring 3, Key Stakeholders, and then needed to identify a needed ally who could connect with the guidance counsellor. See Figure 11.2 for a summary of this career educator's strategic connections. Sample key stakeholders relevant to front-line career development practitioners in various contexts are listed in Figure 11.3.

Figure 11.2. **Rings of influence for a sample career educator.** An example of a career educator's inside-out engagement strategy for incorporating mental health (MH) outcomes in a career development (CD) course.

Context	Career Development Practitioner	Key Stakeholders
Employment Agency	Employment Counsellor	• Executive Director/CEO
Government Department	Employment Counsellor	• Executive Director • Deputy Minister • Assistant Deputy Minister
Primary or Secondary School	Career Educator	• Principal • Assistant or Vice-Principal • Head of Guidance • Parent Council Chair
Post-Secondary Educational Institution	Career Services Advisor	• Career Centre Director • Student Services Director
Human Resources (HR) Department	HR Generalist	• Director, HR • Vice-President, HR

Figure 11.3. Sample key stakeholders in different contexts.

Key Stakeholders

Which individuals have the decision-making authority and/or influence to enable you to pursue your ideas regarding career development and mental health? Which trusted and needed allies can help connect you to these stakeholders? Which new allies should you add to your existing lists?

Iterate and Engage

Be prepared for an iterative process of testing your idea with someone, then changing the idea slightly, and then testing with someone else, and so on. The process becomes less "step by step" at this point and more "go with the flow." You simply cannot know how things will proceed in an engagement strategy. All you can do is get started, recognizing that the back-and-forth nature of the process is essential to successfully reaching and engaging the outer ring.

Be prepared for roadblocks along the way. Engagement efforts can go wrong and do not always work. As you move from the centre outward, you may reach individuals who have other priorities and motivations that simply are not changeable, at least for the moment.

Things can also go right in bigger ways than you were expecting. Every system (e.g., team, department, organization) is a sub-system of another system (e.g., a school is part of a school division; a government employment centre is part of a government department). When mapping out rings of allies and stakeholders, your outer ring will stop with the decision-makers of the immediate system you want to change, such as a school or employment office. If your idea is well-received, key stakeholders in your system may become so engaged that they want to create change in *their* immediate system. A school principal may want the school board to adopt the idea, or an employment centre manager may want to engage all employment centres within the government department with the idea. This will be very good news for you but will almost certainly result in you losing control of the idea. However, true engagement actually requires a loss of control: Ideally, stakeholders should feel as though it is *their* idea for which *they* have a voice and some control.

Thus far we have described the need and a process for vertical engagement within an organization or system's hierarchy. Inside-out engagement can work horizontally or laterally as well, however. In this section, we address the engagement of mental health professionals in understanding and exploring career development and mental health connections. We do so because our two professions, and the individuals working in them, are aligned at the level of "heart." We both will benefit from working together to effectively support our respective clients.

There is another reason to engage mental health professionals in particular. The evidence suggests that it is only a matter of time until the broader network of stakeholders in communities, educational systems, organizations, and local, regional, and national governments comes to realize both that career development practitioners do work that contributes to positive mental health and that career development intervention is, in fact, mental health intervention. Mental health practitioners are themselves a highly varied group comprising individuals with varied professional and non-professional designations including counsellors, social workers, psychologists, nurses, physicians, and psychiatrists. They work in equally varied environments, including private-practice settings, community counselling agencies, school and post-secondary counselling departments, regional mental health clinics, and hospitals. We can all envision the possibility of an important reciprocal relationship with mental health practitioners as career development practitioners are increasingly recognized for the mental health outcomes their work creates.

At your best, you are working within your boundaries of competence, addressing concerns that fall within your role, and being properly resourced and supported to provide the services you do. As a career development practitioner, you will never be responsible for assessing and intervening directly with mental health concerns unless you have adequate training and it is in your role to do so. You will, however, meet with clients whom you feel might benefit from direct support for their mental health concerns, especially when you are actively raising awareness of mental health and communicating the wellbeing benefits of your work. This scenario is easy to imagine and has probably happened countless times. Now, imagine a reciprocal scenario wherein a mental health practitioner is working with a client to intervene directly with a mental health concern or mental illness condition such as depression, anxiety, substance use disorder, attentional concern, or autism. Now imagine that this practitioner is aware of how the positive mental health outcomes associated with career development intervention can benefit their client. It is easy to imagine, but at this point it seldom happens because mental health practitioners are mostly unaware of this aspect of our practice.

The ultimate truth here is that our professions need each other. Career development practitioners need appropriate access and easy paths to refer clients who might benefit from direct support for mental health concerns and mental illness conditions. Mental health practitioners and services need the career development profession to augment and support their mental health intervention. It is the right direction and outcome for at least some clients to receive services from each profession. Moreover, we are ethically obliged to find a way to collaborate with and/or refer to practitioners in the other profession. The evidence points to this obligation in the spirit of providing the best service to our respective clients. This idea speaks to the "heart" for both professions; we both care and we both want to provide the best service and create the best outcomes for our clients.

Key Considerations

Career development practitioners and mental health professionals care deeply about the welfare, health, happiness, and wellbeing of the clients they serve. Beyond this common ground, both professions share many similarities:

- Both are helping professions focused on serving clients and meeting needs.
- Both use interpersonal skills and the client/practitioner relationship as intervention and to deliver intervention.
- Both are guided by codes of ethics and standards of behaviour focused on protecting clients and ensuring effective intervention.
- Both are focused on wellbeing.
- Both use some of the same language to talk about their clients and the types of concerns clients present with.

These overt similarities can lead to concerns about overlap in services, service mandates, types of interventions, and intervention outcomes. To collaborate effectively for the sake of their clients, members of each profession must be clear about their boundaries of competence and areas of expertise. In communicating with mental health professional, career development practitioners should be very clear about the following.

- **Mandate.** Career development practitioners work with clients to provide career development intervention. Mental health outcomes are produced as a positive side effect of attending to this mandate. Mental health practitioners are focused on producing mental health outcomes.

- **Terminology.** It is best for career development practitioners to refer to themselves as, well, career development practitioners and to describe what they do as career development intervention. They can refer to the specific things they do, such as guided self-assessment, resumé development, or interview skills training, but also describe, if possible, the positive mental health mechanisms associated with that work, using the language/terminology of career development. These would include some of the effects (e.g., opportunity perceptions) or coping outcomes (e.g., increased sense of being able to cope). Doing so would make it clear that career development practitioners are not aiming directly at mental health outcomes but are supporting clients in coping with important career-related demands.

- **Nature or type of services.** The type and nature of services provided are highly variable and depend on the context (e.g., a one-time 30-minute meeting or regular meetings over a number of weeks). Career development intervention is perceived as "helping," therefore it is probably important to be clear about the type of service and nature of contact with clients.

Despite different mandates, interests, and foci (different "heads"), as professions (and likely as people), career development practitioners and mental health professionals are greatly aligned in terms of what they care about (similar "hearts"). Including mental health practitioners in your circle of allies and stakeholders will benefit by communicating first and foremost about the heart of the matter.

Who Are Your Mental Health Stakeholders?

In determining your key mental-health-professional stakeholders, it is useful to think in terms of the path(s) clients might take to find mental health support. Anyone, including career development practitioners, can refer a client facing imminent risk to an emergency service such as a regional mental health clinic or a hospital. These emergency services are not the best candidates for your networking. They tend to not engage in longer-term, developmental services. Instead, they provide a quick, but vital, safety-oriented intervention that usually includes referral to other services. A grassroots approach that has you building relationships with clinics and agencies in your community will yield greater gains.

Mental health professionals working in an agency or clinic meet regularly to consult about their clients' needs, including referral (some private practitioners do this as well). Such meetings are intended to determine how best to meet the needs of the clients being served, and provide concrete and social support to the mental health practitioners. Clients who would benefit from the tangible and positive mental health benefits of career development intervention are discussed regularly at the meetings. Your key mental-health-practitioner stakeholders will be the clinic directors, supervisors, and possibly front-line therapists working in these agencies. The inside-out engagement strategy will work perfectly to secure an audience with these people, where you can share with them at the level of heart and find ways to collaborate effectively to meet the needs of the clients you both serve. This approach will lead to referral to, and utilization of, your career development services. As we mentioned earlier, a solid relationship with a mental health practitioner or agency will also greatly increase the likelihood of effective referrals to their services.

Summary

In this chapter, we outlined a practitioner-centred approach to expanding your circle of influence to include key allies and stakeholders in your professional and expanded community. The key benefit of the approach is that it lends itself to integration in the day-to-day functioning of front-line career development practitioners. In addition to educational and marketing benefits, inside-out engagement will likely support effective collaboration and referral between two heart-aligned groups of professionals: career development and mental health practitioners.

Reflection Questions

1. How might you use the inside-out approach to make change in your community, hobby group, family, or place of worship?

2. What barriers might you encounter in incorporating mental health more explicitly at work? How might you find out how real, strong, and unchangeable (or how illusory, weak, and changeable!) these barriers are?

3. What, if anything, prevents or impedes you from influencing others at work? What is one thing you could learn that might lessen your hesitation? How might you engage in this learning?

Never doubt that a small group of thoughtful, committed citizens can change the world. Indeed, it is the only thing that ever has.

Margaret Mead

To Ponder...

When you think about your legacy as a career development practitioner, what do you envision? How would you like to be known by clients or students and colleagues?

12. Conclusion: Now Is the Time

Career development produces mental health outcomes. Intentional career development, the kind that career development practitioners aim for with their interventions, reliably generates positive mental health outcomes, directly and indirectly. Career development interventions help individuals obtain work, become more capable, see themselves differently, and see the world differently. Each of these effects leads to mental health outcomes. Furthermore, these effects change how the world sees and treats individuals, revealing opportunities that would otherwise remain hidden. Capitalizing on these opportunities creates a new cycle of career development effects—obtaining better work, becoming even more capable, perceiving oneself more clearly and positively, and seeing the world more broadly and optimistically—resulting in the world revealing new opportunities to the individual, further contributing to positive mental health outcomes.

Career development interventions, of which there are many, each contribute in different ways to parts of an individual's overall career development. Virtually all career development interventions, however, improve stress control, usually by addressing perceived inequities between demands and coping capacity. Career development interventions help individuals cope with significant demands they face. More importantly, career development interventions help individuals deal with the sources of their stress (stressors), not only the symptoms of stress. Career development interventions do this by helping individuals reduce the demands they face, increase their ability to handle the demands (coping skills), or both. Furthermore, career development interventions cultivate coping skills that can be used with future similar and related demands, thereby averting or limiting future stress. Career development intervention—the set of activities from which you draw—leads to increased client perceptions about coping with important present and future demands and thus converts coping into hope.

Most definitions of mental health include the Public Health Agency of Canada's (2014) notion that it includes "the capacity of each and all of us to feel, think, act in ways that enhance our ability to enjoy life and deal with the challenges we face." This quote describes, at a minimum, coping. In its full manifestation, it also describes an individual moving toward a preferred future, the overarching aim of career development.

Sometimes coping is not possible because options for either reducing demands or bolstering coping capacity are unavailable. Such is the case with mental illness; its effects and forces are at times beyond an individual's control. Career development intervention does not treat mental illness and the career development field makes no claims in this regard. However, in strengthening mental health, career development intervention can increase personal protective factors that can mitigate mental illness and improve the quality of life for those experiencing and coping with mental illness. In other words, when your intervention contributes to client "flourishing" rather than "languishing" (Westerhof & Keyes, 2010), you are helping clients create the conditions whereby mental illness is less likely to be triggered (or, if present, less likely to generate symptoms) and the duration of symptoms, when they appear, is more likely to be shortened.

The contributions of career development intervention to mental health can be achieved ethically and within the boundaries of one's competence, role, and resources. Career development practitioners do not need to step out of their roles to make these contributions. The effects we describe in this book are *already* being achieved by career development intervention. Our recommendations for practice centre on two areas. One is becoming more intentional about attending to the effects. The other area, the one we devoted most attention to, is being cognizant of coping with stress when working with clients so that interventions more explicitly address (1) reducing the demands they face (e.g., "You're feeling like you should know what you're going to be doing five years from now and that something's wrong with you because you don't. I'd like you to know that most students at your grade level don't know and can't know; you are not at all alone in not knowing." and (2) helping develop the skills needed to cope with these demands (e.g., resumé writing, study skills).

Career development practitioners focus on career-related demands and clients seek their help specifically for these demands. The evidence is clear, however, that managing career-related demands can have a global impact on a client's wellbeing. Career development practitioners owe it to clients and students to let them know about this impact. We used the core structuring skill of information giving as an appropriate way of doing this.

The ideas and research described in this book do not change the fact that mental illness is common and can have an enormous impact on all aspects of career development. Nothing presented here changes the need for career development practitioners to take into account the impact of mental illness, have interpersonal skills that support clients to reveal the need for additional help, and make appropriate referrals to mental health professionals. By being more conscious of and transparent about mental health, however, we believe career development practitioners will be better positioned to make clients more receptive to discussing mental illness concerns and the impact of these concerns on career development.

A problem we repeatedly mentioned throughout the book is the lack of evidence-gathering that we in the field of career development engage in, particularly with regard to mental health outcomes. It should not be difficult to make the case that career development intervention produces outcomes above and beyond employment or entry into training/ education, but currently the supporting data are not there. We trust that the Post-Pre Assessment items we provided are sufficiently easy to administer and score that the field can begin to collect these data across a wide variety of regions, contexts, and client/student demographics. We also hope that career development practitioners will use the ideas and questions we provided to ask their clients about the broader impact of career development interventions.

Of course, evidence will have little collective power until all of us in the career development field more skilfully, strategically, and sustainably communicate the value of our work to others. We collectively teach clients to differentiate their value, determine their offerings, create elevator speeches, and document their successes, yet this promotional prowess does not seem to be our field's gift. Wendy Fox, a seasoned career development practitioner, used to tell clients: "It used to be that the phrase 'It's not what you know, it's who you know' was true for job seekers. Then it was 'It's not who you know, it's what you know.' Now, it's 'Who knows what you know?'" (personal communication). This idea holds true for our field as well. If no one knows what we know, do, and achieve, it will be difficult to gain the support and attention we need to obtain sufficient resources to do quality work, engage in research to advance our base of evidence, or develop ourselves at the pace the labour market and our clients require. We know this takes concerted effort, capacity development, and time. We firmly believe the dividends will be great if we make this investment as a field.

Of course, we are not the first to think about career development as mental health intervention; several authors have tried to push this idea forward over the last five or six decades. We wrote this book in part because these authors' efforts have not been sustained. Their work will not have been in vain, however, if we seize the opportunity that societal interest in mental health is affording us at this moment. People are interested in mental health, and now is the time to show them how we contribute to positive mental health, to generate better evidence of these contributions, and to improve our contributions.

A Call to Action

We are determined to generate sustainable momentum regarding research, concept development, and practice improvements with regard to career development and mental health. This will require a much bigger community than "Dave and Michael"!

We have started a small and very informal community of practice (CoP) for those interested in the topic. Currently, belonging to the Career Development and Mental Health CoP involves being on an email list and receiving a monthly or biweekly email on the topic. These emails will eventually morph into a blog to which interested members of the CoP will be welcome to contribute.

The intention with the CoP is to keep the conversation about career development and mental health going. We believe this can be done by sharing ideas, research findings, promising practices, and evaluation methods that will not only improve the field's ability to impact mental health but will improve the career development field overall.

If you are interested in being part of the CoP, please indicate this in an email to Dave Redekopp, liferole@telusplanet.net. You can opt out any time.

We are committed to this initiative and welcome any and all ongoing input. If you would like to receive periodic updates on our work, or if you would simply like to send information our way, please get in touch with Dave.

Reflection Questions

1. Looking back on the whole book, what is a key takeaway that could bolster your own mental health? What will you do to ensure this takeaway *does* bolster your mental health?

2. What is the single most likely change the ideas in this book might prompt you to make? What will you do to ensure that you make this change?

3. What single learning will the ideas in this book most likely prompt you to undertake? What will you do to ensure that you undertake this learning?

About That Request

In Chapter 1, we invited you to complete a short evaluation of this book in service of improving the second edition as well as other resources on this topic. We thank you again for investing your time and energy in reading this book, and remind you that the evaluation is available at www.life-role.com/CDMH.htm. Thank you in advance!

References

Achor, S. (2010). *The happiness advantage: The seven principles of positive psychology that fuel success and performance at work.* New York: Penguin Random House.

Aiello, A., & Tesi, A. (2017). Psychological well-being and work engagement among Italian social workers: Examining the mediational role of job resources. *Social Work Research, 41*(2), 73–84. https://doi.org/10.1093/swr/svx005

Akkermans, J., Brenninkmeijer, V., Schaufeli, W., & Blonk, R. (2015). It's all about CareerSKILLS: Effectiveness of a career development intervention for young employees. *Human Resource Management, 54*(4), 533–551. https://doi.org/10.1002/hrm.21633

American Psychiatric Association. (2013). *Diagnostic and statistical manual of mental disorders: DSM–5* (5th ed.). Washington, DC: American Psychiatric Association.

Amundson, N. E., Goddard, T., Niles, S. G., Yoon, H. J., & Schmidt, J. (2016). *Hope centred career interventions research project: Final report.* Toronto, ON: CERIC.

Antonovsky, A. (1987). *Unraveling the mystery of health: How people manage stress and stay well.* San Francisco, CA: Jossey-Bass.

Australian Bureau of Statistics. (2007). *National survey of mental health and wellbeing: Summary of results.* [Catalogue No. 4326.0)]. Canberra, Australia: Australian Bureau of Statistics.

Australian Bureau of Statistics. (2017). *Underlying cause of death in Australia.* Canberra, Australia: Australian Bureau of Statistics.

Australian Government Department of Health. (2008). National mental health policy 2008: Glossary. Retrieved from https://www1.health.gov.au/internet/publications/publishing.nsf/Content/mental-pubs-n-pol08-toc~mental-pubs-n-pol08-3 on September 21, 2019.

Australian Government Department of Health and Ageing. (2003). National Mental Health Plan 2003–2008. Retrieved from https://www.aph.gov.au/Parliamentary_Business/Committees/Senate/Former_Committees/mentalhealth/report/e01 on September 21, 2019.

Australian Government National Mental Health Commission. (2016). Economics of mental health in Australia. Retrieved from https://www.mentalhealthcommission.gov.au/news/2016/december/economics-of-mental-health-in-australia.

Australian Institute of Health and Welfare. (2018). Health expenditure Australia 2016–17. *Health and welfare expenditure series no. 64.* (Catalogue No. HWE 74). Canberra, Australia: AIHW.

Bandura, A. (1986). *Social foundations of thought and action: A social cognitive theory.* Englewood Cliffs, NJ: Prentice-Hall, Inc.

Bezanson, L., Goyer L., Michaud G., Redekopp, D. E., & Savard, R. (2014). *Transforming the culture of evaluation in career development services.* Paper presented at the World Conference of the International Association of Educational and Vocational Guidance, Quebec City, QC, Canada.

Bloom, D. E., Cafiero, E. T., Jané-Llopis, E., Abrahams-Gessel, S., Bloom, L. R., Fathima, S., . . . Weinstein, C. (2011). *The global economic burden of non-communicable diseases.* Geneva: World Economic Forum.

Boychuk, C., Lysaght, R., & Stuart, H. (2018). Career decision-making processes of young adults with first-episode psychosis. *Qualitative Health Research, 28*(6), 1016–1031. https://doi.org/10.1177/1049732318761864

Brand, J. E. (2015). The far-reaching impact of job loss and unemployment. *Annual Review of Sociology, 41*(1), 359–375. https://doi.org/10.1146/annurev-soc-071913-043237

Bright, J., & Pryor, R. (2011). The chaos theory of careers. *Journal of Employment Counseling, 48*(4), 163–166. https://doi.org/10.1002/j.2161-1920.2011.tb01104.x

Brown, D., & Brooks, L. (1985). Career counseling as a mental health intervention. *Professional Psychology: Research and Practice, 16*(6), 860–867. https://doi.org/10.1037/0735-7028.16.6.860

Canadian Standards and Guidelines for Career Development Practitioners (2012). Glossary of terms. Retrieved from http://career-dev-guidelines.org/career_dev/wp-content/uploads/2015/06/Glossary.pdf on September 25, 2018.

Cannon, W. B. (1929). Bodily changes in pain, hunger, fear and rage. *Southern Medical Journal, 22*(9), 870. https://doi.org/10.1097/00007611-192909000-00037

Caporoso, R. A., & Kiselica, M. S. (2004). Career counseling with clients who have a severe mental illness. *The Career Development Quarterly, 52*(3), 235–245. https://doi.org/10.1002/j.2161-0045.2004.tb00645.x

Career Education Assocation of Victoria. (2019). Definition of career development. Retrieved from https://www.ceav.vic.edu.au/career-development/definition-of-career-development/

Career Industry Council of Australia. (2019). Professional standards for Australian development practitioners. Retrieved from https://cica.org.au/wp-content/uploads/Professional-Standards-for-Australian-Career-Development-Practitioners-2019.pdf

Carkhuff, R. R. (1969). *Helping and human relations: A primer for lay and professional helpers* (Vols. 1–2). New York: Holt, Rinehart and Winston.

Centre for Addiction and Mental Health. (2019). Mental illness and addiction: Facts and statistics. Retrieved from https://www.camh.ca/en/driving-change/the-crisis-is-real/mental-health-statistics

Centre for Chronic Disease Prevention. (2016). Positive mental health surveillance indicator framework: Quick statistics, adults (18 years of age and older) Canada, 2016 Edition. Ottawa, ON: Public Health Agency of Canada. Retrieved from http://www.phac-aspc.gc.ca/publicat/hpcdp-pspmc/36-1/assets/pdf/ar-02-eng.pdf

Chan, R., Shum, D., Toulopoulou, T., & Chen, E. (2008). Assessment of executive functions: Review of instruments and identification of critical issues. *Archives of Clinical Neuropsychology, 23*(2), 201–216. https://doi.org/10.1016/j.acn.2007.08.010

Chase-Lansdale, P., Sabol, T., Sommer, T., Chor, E., Cooperman, A., Brooks-Gunn, J., ... Morris, A. (2019). Effects of a two-generation human capital program on low-income parents' education, employment, and psychological wellbeing. *Journal of Family Psychology, 33*(4), 433–443. https://doi.org/10.1037/fam0000517

Chopra, D. (2009). *The ultimate happiness prescription: 7 keys to joy and enlightenment.* New York: Harmony.

Clarke, A., Amundson, N., Niles, S., & Yoon, H. J. (2018). Action-oriented hope: an agent of change for internationally educated professionals. Retrieved from http://perspectives2017.com/wp-content/uploads/2017/03/Action-oriented-Hope-An-Agent-of-Change-for-Internationally-Educated-Professionals.pdf

Dalai Lama, Tutu, D., & Abrams, D. (2016). *The book of joy: Lasting happiness in a changing world.* New York: Viking.

Deci, E. L., & Ryan, R. M. (2000). The "what" and "why" of goal pursuits: Human needs and the self-determination of behavior. *Psychological Inquiry, 11*(4), 227–268. https://doi.org/10.1207/S15327965PLI1104_01

Dewa, C. S., Chau, N., & Dermer, S. (2010). Examining the comparative incidence and costs of physical and mental health-related disabilities in an employed population. *Journal of Occupational and Environmental Medicine, 52*(7), 758–762. https://doi.org/10.1097/JOM.0b013e3181e8cfb5

Diener, E., & Biswas-Diener, R. (2008). *Happiness: Unlocking the mysteries of psychological wealth.* Malden, MA: Blackwell.

Duffy, R., Douglass, R., Autin, K., & Allan, B. (2014). Examining predictors and outcomes of a career calling among undergraduate students. *Journal of Vocational Behavior, 85*(3), 309–318. https://doi.org/10.1016/j.jvb.2014.08.009

Duncan, B. L., Miller, S. D., Wampold, B. E., & Hubble, M. A. (2010). *The heart and soul of change: Delivering what works in therapy.* Washington, D.C. American Psychological Association.

Dweck, C. S. (1999). *Self-theories: Their role in motivation, personality, and development.* Philadelphia, PA: Psychology Press.

Egan, G. (2014). *The skilled helper: A problem-management and opportunity-development approach to helping* (10th ed.). Belmont, CA: Brooks/Cole, Cengage Learning.

Epstein, R. (2011). Fight the frazzled mind: Proactive steps manage stress. *Scientific American Mind, 22*(4), 30. https://doi.org/10.1038/scientificamericanmind0911-30

Faragher, E. B., Cass, M., & Cooper, C. L. (2005). The relationship between job satisfaction and health: A meta-analysis. *Occupational and Environmental Medicine, 62*(2), 105–112. https://doi.org/10.1136/oem.2002.006734

Frederickson, B. L. (2004). The broaden-and-build theory of positive emotions. *Philosophical Transactions of the Royal Society B: Biological Sciences.* https://doi.org/10.1098/rstb.2004.1512

Galderisi, S., Heinz, A., Kastrup, M., Beezhold, J., & Sartorius, N. (2015). Toward a new definition of mental health. *World Psychiatry, 14*(2), 231–233. https://doi.org/10.1002/wps.20231

Gelatt, H. B., & Gelatt, C. (2003). *Creative decision-making using positive uncertainty.* Boston, MA: Thompson Learning.

Ginevra, M., & Nota, L. (2018). "Journey in the world of professions and work": A career intervention for children. *The Journal of Positive Psychology, 13*(5), 460–470. https://doi.org/10.1080/17439760.2017.1303532

Ginzberg, E., Ginsburg, S., Axelrad, S, & Herma, J. (1951). *Occupational choice: An approach to a general theory.* New York, NY: Columbia Univeristy Press

Glerum, J., Loyens, S. M. M., & Rikers, R. M. J. P. (2018). Is an online mindset intervention effective in vocational education? *Journal of Interactive Learning Environments.* https://doi.org/10.1080/10494820.2018.1552877

Greenberg, J. S. (2013). *Comprehensive stress management* (13th ed.). New York, NY: McGraw-Hill.

Gurung, R. A. R., & Roethel-Wendorf, A. (2009). Stress and mental health. In *Culture and mental health: Sociocultural influences, theory, and practice* (pp. 35–53). West Sussex, UK: John Wiley & Sons.

Haché, L., Redekopp, D., & Jarvis, P. (2006). *Blueprint for life/work designs.* Memramcook, NB: National Life/Work Centre.

Hanh, T. N. (2005). *Happiness: Essential mindfulness practices.* Berkeley, CA: Parallax Press.

Harnois, G., & Gabriel, P. (2000). *Mental health and work: Impact, issues and good practices.* Retrieved from https://apps.who.int/iris/handle/10665/42346

Harvey, S., Joyce, S., Modini, M., Christensen, H., Bryant, R., Mykletun, A., & Mitchell, P. B. (2013). *Work and depression/anxiety disorders: A systematic review of reviews.* Retrieved from https://www.beyondblue.org.au/docs/default-source/research-project-files/bw0204.pdf?sfvrsn=4

Harvey, S., Modini, M., Joyce, S., Milligan-Saville, J., Tan, L., Mykletun, A., ... Mitchell, P. (2017). Can work make you mentally ill? A systematic meta-review of work-related risk factors for common mental health problems. *Occupational and Environmental Medicine, 74*(4), 301.

Herr, E. L. (1989). Career development and mental health. *Journal of Career Development, 16*(1), 5–18. https://doi.org/10.1177/089484538901600102

Hiebert, B. (1988). Controlling stress: A conceptual update. *Canadian Journal of Counselling and Psychotherapy, 22*(4), 226–241. Retrieved from http://cjc-rcc.ucalgary.ca/cjc/index.php/rcc/article/view/1321

Hiebert, B., & Magnusson, K. (2014). The power of evidence: Demonstrating the value of career development services. In B. C. Shepard & P. S. Mani (Eds.), *Career development practice in Canada: Perspectives, principles, and professionalism* (pp. 489–530). Toronto, ON: CERIC.

Hill, C. E. (2014). *Helping skills: Facilitating exploration, insight, and action* (4th ed.). Washington, DC: American Psychological Association.

Hillman, J. (1975). *Re-visioning psychology.* New York: Harper & Row.

Hirschi, A., Abessolo, M., & Froidevaux, A. (2015). Hope as a resource for career exploration: Examining incremental and cross-lagged effects. *Journal of Vocational Behavior, 86,* 38–47.

Holland, J. L. (1973). *Making vocational choices*. Englewood Cliffs, NJ: Prentice Hall.

Holland, J. L. (1997). *Making vocational choices: A theory of vocational personalities and work environments*. Lutz, FL: Psychological Assessment Resources.

Holmes, T., & Rahe, R. (1967). The social readjustment rating scale. *Journal of Psychosomatic Research, 11*(2), 213–218. https://doi.org/10.1016/0022-3999(67)90010-4

Huston, M., & Dobbs, J. (2014). Making the case for career development as a mental health intervention: A literature review with some interesting findings. Paper presented at the Annual Conference of the Canadian Association of College and University Student Services, Halifax, Nova Scotia, Canada.

Index Mundi. (2019). Country comparison – population. Retrieved from https://www.indexmundi.com/g/r.aspx?t=50&v=21&l=en

Ivey, A. E., Ivey, M. B., & Zalaquette, C. P. (2010). *Intentional interviewing and counseling: Facilitating client development in a multicultural society* (7th ed.). Pacific Grove, CA: Brooks/Cole.

Jahoda, M. (1959). Current concepts of positive mental health. *The American Journal of the Medical Sciences, 238*(1), 527. https://doi.org/10.1097/00000441-195910000-00026

Jahoda, M. (1981). Work, employment, and unemployment: Values, theories, and approaches in social research. *American Psychologist, 36*(2), 184-191. doi:10.1037/0003-066X.36.2.184

Johnson, S. (2019). The graduate wellbeing questions are an accident waiting to happen [Blog post]. Retrieved from https://wonkhe.com/blogs/the-graduate-wellbeing-questions-are-an-accident-waiting-to-happen/

Joyce, S., Modini, M., Christensen, H., Mykletun, A., Bryant, R., Mitchell, P. B., & Harvey, S. B. (2016). Workplace interventions for common mental disorders: A systematic meta-review. *Psychological medicine, 46*(4), 683. https://doi.org/10.1017/S0033291715002408

Kerr, B., & Robinson Kurpius, S. (2004). Encouraging talented girls in math and science: Effects of a guidance intervention. *High Ability Studies, 15*(1), 85–102. https://doi.org/10.1080/1359813042000225357

Kessler, C. R., Amminger, P. G., Aguilar-Gaxiola, B. S., Alonso, B. J., Lee, B. S., & Üstün, B. T. (2007). Age of onset of mental disorders: A review of recent literature. *Current Opinion in Psychiatry, 20*(4), 359–364. https://doi.org/10.1097/YCO.0b013e32816ebc8c

Keyes, C. L. M. (2005). Mental illness and/or mental health? Investigating axioms of the complete state model of health. *Journal of Consulting and Clinical Psychology, 73*(3), 539–548. https://doi.org/10.1037/0022-006X.73.3.539

Keyes, C. L. M. (2006). Mental health in adolescence: Is America's youth flourishing? *American Journal of Orthopsychiatry, 76*(3), 395–402. https://doi.org/10.1037/0002-9432.76.3.395

Keyes, C. L. M. (2014). Mental health as a complete state: How the salutogenic perspective completes the picture. In G.F. Bauer & O. Hammig (Eds.), *Bridging occupational, organizational and public health: A transdisciplinary approach.* New York: Springer.

Keyes, C. L. M., Wissing, M., Potgieter, J. P., Temane, M., Kruger, A., & Van Rooy, S. (2008). Evaluation of the mental health continuum–short form (MHC–SF) in setswana-speaking South Africans. *Clinical Psychology & Psychotherapy, 15*(3), 181–192. https://doi.org/10.1002/cpp.572

Lankard, B. A. (1991). *Strategies for implementing the National Career Development Guidelines. ERIC Digest No. 117.* Columbus, OH: ERIC Clearinghouse on Adult Career and Vocational Education.

Lazarus, R. S., & Folkman, S. (1984). *Stress, appraisal, and coping.* New York, NY: Springer.

Lengelle, R., Luken, T., & Meijers, F. (2016). Is self-reflection dangerous? Preventing rumination in career learning. *Australian Journal of Career Development, 25*(3), 99–109.

Lewis, N. A., Turiano, N. A., Payne, B. R., & Hill, P. L. (2017). Purpose in life and cognitive functioning in adulthood. *Aging, Neuropsychology, and Cognition, 24*(6), 662–671. https://doi.org/10.1080/13825585.2016.1251549

Li, F., Chen, J., Yu, L., Jing, Y., Jiang, P., Fu, X., ... Liu, Y. (2016). The role of stress management in the relationship between purpose in life and self-rated health in teachers: A mediation analysis. *International Journal of Environmental Research and Public Health, 13*(7). https://doi.org/10.3390/ijerph13070719

Luciano, A., & Carpenter-Song, E. A. (2014). A qualitative study of career exploration among young adult men with psychosis and co-occurring substance use disorder. *Journal of Dual Diagnosis, 10*(4), 220–225. https://doi.org/10.1080/15504263.2014.962337

Martin, J., & Hiebert, B. A. (1985). *Instructional counseling: A method for counselors.* Pittsburgh, PA: University of Pittsburgh Press.

Mental Health Commission of Canada. (2011). *The Life and Economic Impact of Major Mental Illnesses in Canada.* Ottawa, ON: Author.

Mental Health Commission of Canada. (2013). *Making the Case for Investing in Mental Health in Canada.* Ottawa, ON: Author.

Mullainathan, S., & Shafir, E. (2013). *Scarcity: Why having too little means so much.* New York, NY: Henry Holt & Company.

Neary, S., Dodd, V., & Hooley, T. (2015). *Understanding career management skills: Findings from the first phase of the CMS LEADER project.* Derby, UK: International Centre for Guidance Studies, University of Derby.

Niles, S. G., Amundson, N., & Neault, R. (2011). *Career flow: A hope-centred approach to career development.* Columbus, OH: Pearson, Merrill Prentice Hall.

Niles, S. G., Amundson, N., & Yoon, H.J. (2019). Hope-action theory: Creating and sustaining hope in career development. In N. Arthur, R. Neault, & M. McMahon (Eds.), *Career theories and models at work: Ideas for practice* (pp. 283–293). Toronto: CERIC.

Noone, P. A. (2017). The Holmes-Rahe Stress Inventory. *Occupational medicine (Oxford, England), 67*(7), 581. https://doi.org/10.1093/occmed/kqx099

Park, M. (2013). Evidence-based stress management: Focusing on nonpharmacological procedure which reduce stress and promote health. *Journal of the Korean Medical Association, 56*(6), 478–484. https://doi.org/10.5124/jkma.2013.56.6.478

Parsons, F. (1909). *Choosing a vocation.* Boston: Houghton Mifflin.

Pearson, C., Janz, T., & Ali, J. (2013). Mental and substance use disorders in Canada. Health at a glance. Statistics Canada Catalogue no. 82-624-X. Retrieved from https://www150.statcan.gc.ca/n1/pub/82-624-x/2013001/article/11855-eng.htm on September 19, 2019.

Peck, H. I. (1975). *Annual evaluation report for the exemplary project in career development, 1975*. ERIC. Retrieved from https://eric.ed.gov/?id=ED152780

Petrie, K., Joyce, S., Tan, L., Henderson, M., Johnson, A., Nguyen, H., ... Harvey, S. B. (2018). A framework to create more mentally healthy workplaces: A viewpoint. *Australian & New Zealand Journal of Psychiatry, 52*(1), 15–23. https://doi.org/10.1177/0004867417726174

Plait, P. (2018). The secret to making scientific discoveries? Making mistakes [Video]. Retrieved from https://www.ted.com/talks/phil_plait_the_secret_to_scientific_discoveries_making_mistakes?language=en

Prochaska, J. O., & DiClemente, C. C. (1983). Stages and processes of self-change of smoking: Toward an integrative model of change. *Journal of Consulting and Clinical Psychology, 51*(3), 390–395. https://doi.org/10.1037/0022-006X.51.3.390

Public Health Agency of Canada. (2014). Mental health promotion. Retrieved from https://www.canada.ca/en/public-health/services/health-promotion/mental-health/mental-health-promotion.html on September 21, 2019.

Raskin, J. D. (2018). What might an alternative to the DSM suitable for psychotherapists look like? *Journal of Humanistic Psychology, 59*(3), 368–375. https://doi.org/10.1177/0022167818761919

Redekopp, D. E., Bezanson, L., & Dugas, T. (2013). *Common indicators: Transforming the culture of evaluation in career development and employment services*. Ottawa, ON: Canadian Career Development Foundation.

Redekopp, D. E., Bezanson, L., & Dugas, T. (2015). *Evidence-based employment services: Common indicators. Phase II final research report*. Ottawa, ON: Canadian Career Development Foundation.

Redekopp, D. E., & Crickmore, C. (1996). Workability handbook. *NATCON Proceedings*. Toronto, ON: University of Toronto Career Centre.

Redekopp, D. E., & Huston, M. (2018). The broader aims of career development: Mental health, wellbeing and work. *British Journal of Guidance and Counselling, 47*(2), 246–257. doi:10.1080/0306 9885.2018.1513451

Rhew, E., Piro, J. S., Goolkasian, P., & Cosentino, P. (2018). The effects of a growth mindset on self-efficacy and motivation. *Cogent Education, 5*(1), 16. https://doi.org/10.1080/233118 6X.2018.1492337

Ritchie, H., & Roser, M. (2018). Mental health. Retrieved from Our World in Data website https://ourworldindata.org/mental-health

Robertson, P. J. (2013). The well-being outcomes of career guidance. *British Journal of Guidance & Counselling, 41*(3), 254–266. https://doi.org/10.1080/03069885.2013.773959

Ryan, R. M. (1995). Psychological needs and the facilitation of integrative processes. *Journal of personality, 63*(3), 397–427.

Ryff, C. D. (1989). Happiness is everything, or is it? Explorations on the meaning of psychological well-being. *Journal of Personality and Social Psychology, 57*(6), 1069.

Sainsbury, R., Irvine, A., Aston, J., Wilson, S., Williams, C., & Sinclair, A. (2008). Mental health and employment. York, UK: University of York.

Santilli, S., Nota, L., & Hartung, P. (2019). Efficacy of a group career construction intervention with early adolescent youth (Report). *Journal of Vocational Behavior, 111*, 49–58. https://doi.org/10.1016/j.jvb.2018.06.007

Savickas, M. L. (2011). *Career counseling.* Washington, D.C.: American Psychological Association.

Schnirer, L., Dalton, A., Dennis, D., Hartnagel, T., Galambos, N., & Bisanz, J. (2007). *Capacity building as crime prevention: Outcomes evaluation of the Kids in the Hall Bistro Program.* Edmonton, AB: University of Alberta.

Seligman, M. E. P. (1990). *Learned optimism: How to change your mind and your life.* New York, NY: Pocket Books.

Seligman, M. E. P. (2012). *Flourish: A visionary new understanding of happiness and well-being.* New York: Simon and Schuster.

Selye, H. (1973). The evolution of the stress concept: The originator of the concept traces its development from the discovery in 1936 of the alarm reaction to modern therapeutic applications of syntoxic and catatoxic hormones. *American Scientist, 61*(6), 692–699.

Snyder, C. R. (2002). Target article: Hope theory: Rainbows in the mind. *Psychological Inquiry, 13*(4), 249–275, https://doi.org/10.1207/S15327965PLI1304_01

Snyder, C. R., Irving, L. M., & Anderson J. (1991). Hope and health. In C. R. Snyder & D. R. Forsyth (Eds.), *Handbook of social and clinical psychology: The health perspective* (pp. 285–305). Elmsford, NY: Pergamon Press.

Spurk, D., Kauffeld, S., Barthauer, L., & Heinemann, N. S. (2015). Fostering networking behavior, career planning and optimism, and subjective career success: An intervention study. *Journal of Vocational Behavior, 87*, 134–144.

Statistics Canada. (2018). Table 13-10-0392-01 Deaths and age-specific mortality rates, by selected grouped causes. Retrieved from https://www150.statcan.gc.ca/t1/tbl1/en/tv.action?pid=1310039201 on September 20, 2019.

Strauser, D., Lustig, D., & Çiftçi, A. (2008). Psychological well-being: Its relation to work personality, vocational identity, and career thoughts. *The Journal of Psychology, 142*(1), 21–35. https://doi.org/10.3200/JRLP.142.1.21-36

Super, D. E. (1957). *The psychology of careers: An introduction to vocational development* (1st ed.). New York and Evanston: Harper & Row.

Szasz, T. (1974). *The myth of mental illness: Foundations of a theory of personal conduct* (Rev. ed.). New York: Harper & Row

Varvogli, L., & Darviri, C. (2011). Stress management techniques: Evidence-based procedures that reduce stress and promote health. *Health Science Journal, 5*(2), 74–89.

Waddell, G., & Burton, A. K. (2006). *Is work good for your health and wellbeing?* Norwich, UK: The Stationary Office.

Westerhof, G. J., & Keyes, C. L. M. (2010). Mental illness and mental health: The two continua model across the lifespan. *Journal of Adult Development, 17*(2), 110–119. https://doi.org/10.1007/s10804-009-9082-y

World Health Organization. (2017). *Depression and other common mental disorders: global health estimates.* Geneva: World Health Organization.

World Health Organization. (2018). Mental health: Mental disorders. Retrieved from https://www.who.int/news-room/fact-sheets/detail/mental-disorders.

World Health Organization. (2019a). Suicide. Retrieved from https://www.who.int/news-room/fact-sheets/detail/suicide.

World Health Organization. (2019b). Mental health: A state of well-being. Retrieved from https://www.who.int/features/factfiles/mental_health/en/ on September 21, 2019.

Wrzesniewski, A., McCauley, C., Rozin, P., & Schwartz, B. (1997). Jobs, careers, and callings: People's relations to their work. *Journal of research in personality, 31*(1), 21–33.

Yerkes, R. M., & Dodson, J. D. (1908). The relation of strength of stimulus to rapidity of habit-formation. *Journal of Comparative Neurology and Psychology, 18*(5), 459–482. https://doi.org/10.1002/cne.920180503

Yoon, H., Bailey, N., Amundson, N., & Niles, S. (2019). The effect of a career development programme based on the Hope-Action Theory: Hope to Work for refugees in British Columbia. *British Journal of Guidance & Counselling, 47*(1), 6–19. https://doi.org/10.1080/03069885.2018.1544827

Yue, X. D., Hiranandani, N. A., Jiang, F., Hou, Z., & Chen, X. (2017). Unpacking the gender differences on mental health: The effects of optimism and gratitude. *Psychological Reports, 120*(4), 639–649. https://doi.org/10.1177/0033294117701136

Zechmann, A., & Paul, K. I. (2019). Why do individuals suffer during unemployment? Analyzing the role of deprived psychological needs in a six-wave longitudinal study. *Journal of Occupational Health Psychology.* https://doi.org/10.1037/ocp0000154

This book has been developed by two long-time Canadian career development practitioners, Dave E. Redekopp and Michael Huston.

Dave is president of the Life-Role Development Group Ltd. and has been an avid champion of career development since 1988. He has received provincial and national awards in career development and is widely recognized in Canada as a thought leader in the field. His career development expertise afforded him the privilege of teaching thousands of practitioners, developing dozens of courses, delivering hundreds of talks, conducting a number of research studies, and developing a host of career development resources for practitioners and the public. Dave holds a PhD in Educational Psychology from the University of Alberta.

Michael has been involved in the career development field as a counsellor, practitioner, trainer, and counsellor educator since the early 1990s. He is a Registered Psychologist, counsellor, and associate professor at Mount Royal University in Calgary, Alberta, Canada, where he provides counselling addressing personal, educational, and career-related concerns. Michael continues to teach graduate courses and facilitate practitioner workshops focused on counselling skills and intervention strategies. His areas of interest and exploration include counsellor training, career intervention, stress and coping, and counselling outcomes and evaluation. He is particularly interested in the various connections between career development, mental health, mental illness, and wellbeing.

Life-Role Development Group Ltd.
NOW | NEXT | FUTURE

The Life-Role Development Group Limited is a Canadian career development firm involved in virtually all aspects of career development, including program, product and service development, career development practitioner training, program delivery, consulting, and research.
life-role.com

A special thank you to our Knowledge Champions for mental health and career development who helped to make possible the publication of this book:

AUSTRALIAN CENTRE FOR CAREER EDUCATION

The Australian Centre for Career Education (ACCE), is a not for profit educational charity. The ACCE has four divisions, CEAV Inc, CEAV Institute, CEAV Career Counselling Australia and CEAV Research and Development, and supports its members to promote career development as a lifelong process. Our purpose is the advancement of career development for public benefit. **ceav.vic.edu.au**

CERIC is a charitable organization that advances education and research in career counselling and career development, in order to increase the economic and social well-being of Canadians. It funds projects to develop innovative resources that build the knowledge and skills of diverse career professionals. CERIC also hosts the Cannexus conference, publishes the Canadian Journal of Career Development and runs the CareerWise / OrientAction websites. **ceric.ca**

Ryerson University is Canada's leader in innovative, career-oriented education. Urban, culturally diverse and inclusive, the university is home to more than 45,300 students, including 2,600 Master's and PhD students, 3,800 faculty and staff, and nearly 198,000 alumni worldwide. For more information, visit **ryerson.ca**

Where innovative education, cutting-edge research, and community outreach intersect, you'll find Simon Fraser University. Our vision? To be Canada's leading engaged university. Founded in 1965, SFU has 30,000 students and 6,500 faculty and staff at three vibrant campuses in the greater Vancouver area, together with more than 160,000 alumni around the world. **sfu.ca**

For over a century, Wilfrid Laurier University has been recognized for academic excellence through diverse, relevant and inspiring programs offered at each of our campus locations – Waterloo, Brantford, Kitchener and Toronto. Pivotal to the Laurier experience is our commitment to engaging all students in their career development as they prepare for the future. **wlu.ca**

It is so refreshing to find a readable and well researched book that integrates theory, research and practice and focuses on the relationship between career development and mental health. Changing economic conditions point towards a future where career goals must include mental health concerns as well as finding suitable work. This broader perspective has been neglected and represents a new vision for our field. The authors, Dave Redekopp and Michael Huston, have created an excellent resource, a book that needs to be on everyone's shelf.

Norman Amundson, Professor Emeritus, University of British Columbia

This guide is a rare and wonderful combination of thoroughly researched, evidence-based information on the inevitable interplay between career development and mental health, with down-to-earth questions, opportunities for reflection, and pragmatic implications for practitioners in the field. Following their own advice, the authors speak both to the head and to the heart of their readers, at once affirming, informing, and challenging us to embrace the wider repercussions and deeper effects that our work in career development has on those we serve. I, for one, gained a greater appreciation for the privilege and the potential of the work we do! What Dave and Michael have created in these pages is an incredible boon to the profession, and I believe it should become required reading for new and seasoned practitioners in the field.

Denise Bissonnette, Career Development Author, Speaker, Trainer, Diversity World

For too long, artificial boundaries have been created between work and mental health in counseling practice, theory, and research. The reality of life is much more complex and nuanced. Dave Redekopp and Michael Huston have written a masterful book that maps the space shared by work and mental health resulting in a game-changing contribution. This book provides a compelling conceptual framework for integrating mental health and career interventions as well as very accessible strategies and tools. This book will quickly become a classic in the field!

David L. Blustein, Professor, Counseling Psychology, Boston College

....

The book provides a significant contribution to our understanding of the key role career development aims and interventions can play in promoting mental health wellbeing and in working with individuals who are experiencing mental health challenges. It also encourages career practitioners to consider the scope and limits of their role, and the skills they need to be effective in working with mental health issues.

William A. Borgen, Professor, Educational and Counselling Psychology, and Special Education, Faculty of Education, University of British Columbia

....

This is a book about human wholeness and interconnectedness. "The hip bone is connected to the thigh bone", work and career are connected to personal and mental well-being. Everything human interrelated. The authors don't let you forget this. Career development is life development.

H B Gelatt, Decision Making Author, Gelatt Partners

This is one of the most promising and encouraging works to come into our field in a very long time. This work demystifies mental health and shows how every practitioner can be a powerful change agent through career development practices. Early in the book, Redekopp and Huston make the assertion that, "As a practitioner who does career development intervention—whether through counselling, teaching, advising, managing, or any other relevant function—you will influence mental health". Given the rising tide of mental health concerns in all walks of life, this is a much needed and most timely assertion. After reading this book, every practitioner will be able to say "I can do this"; because of this book, they will also be highly motivated to do so.

Kris Magnusson, Professor, Faculty of Education, Simon Fraser University

---

The authors combine their extensive experience in career development and mental health counselling to make a compelling case for career development as a mental health intervention. They provide a solid evidence base for the links between intentional career development and better mental health and provide tips for career development practitioners and counsellors to extend that evidence base, join together in a community of practice, and activate their spheres of influence to advocate for career development interventions as a route to improved mental health.

Roberta Neault, President, Life-Strategies Limited

There is a growing recognition of the profound links between work, mental health and well-being. The career development profession has been slow to wake up to the importance of this connection. In this book, Redekopp and Huston have clearly outlined the issues, and explained the implications for career development practitioners in a very accessible way. This is a welcome and long-overdue guide to navigating a challenging dimension of practice.

Peter Robertson, Associate Professor of Career Guidance/Head of Social Sciences, School of Applied Sciences, Edinburgh Napier University

There is a plethora of research evidence that demonstrates the positive impacts that work has on our overall psychological health and wellness - and as a specialist in Psychological Health & Safety (PH&S) in the workplace, I appreciate the focus Dave Redekopp & Michael Huston take in underscoring unique considerations for career development practitioners when it pertains to better understanding the intersection between meaningful work and overall mental heath and wellness.

Dr. Joti Samra, R.Psych., CEO & Founder, MyWorkplaceHealth, Founding and Ongoing Member of the CSA Technical Committee that developed the National Standard of Canada for Psychological Health & Safety in the Workplace (CAN/CSA-Z1003-13/BNQ9700-803/2013)

The ability to work and love are the life roles most deeply connected to one's happiness and satisfaction with life. As Redekopp and Huston explain in this important book, career development interventions address simultaneously the capacity to enact successful careers and satisfying relationships. The authors show how career development practices are indeed mental health interventions and encourage practitioners to both appreciate the mental health aspects of their career services and become more intentional using career interventions that promote the mental health of their students and clients.

Mark Savickas, Professor Emeritus, Northeast Ohio Medical University

Lightning Source UK Ltd.
Milton Keynes UK
UKHW050847160921
390546UK00010B/123